The Border

The Border

The Legacy of a Century of Anglo-Irish Politics

Diarmaid Ferriter

PROFILE BOOKS

First published in Great Britain in 2019 by
Profile Books Ltd
3 Holford Yard
Bevin Way
London WC1X 9HD
www.profilebooks.com

The author and publisher give grateful thanks for the following
extracts: © Paul Muldoon, 1980, *Why Brownlee Left*, Faber & Faber
Ltd; © Seamus Heaney, 1999, 'Terminus', from *Opened Ground:
Selected Poems, 1966–1996*, Faber & Faber Ltd; © Seamus Heaney, 1987,
'Frontier of Writing' from *The Haw Lantern*, Faber & Faber Ltd

1 3 5 7 9 10 8 6 4 2

Typeset in Garamond by MacGuru Ltd
Printed and bound in Great Britain by Clays Ltd, Elcograf S.p.A.

The moral right of the author has been asserted.

A CIP catalogue record for this book is available from the British Library.

ISBN 978 1 78816 178 7
eISBN 978 1 78283 511 0

FSC
www.fsc.org
MIX
Paper from
responsible sources
FSC® C018072

For my beloved brother, Cian

Contents

The Long Gestation

The island of Ireland was partitioned in 1920, partly due to a combination of British duplicity, the insecurities, fears and desires of Ulster unionists and the delusions and dashed hopes of southern Irish republicans and partly because the likely alternative to a border was civil war. In subsequent decades the border was cemented by aggressive political ideology, economic policy and harrowing violence before its potency was tempered by a peace process and economic and political pragmatism. Its future, since the British electorate voted to leave the EU in June 2016, has been under a focus not witnessed in decades, as it is the UK's only land border with another European country.

Ideological partition was long a reality in Ireland before the physical border was imposed owing to the distinctive develop-ment of Ulster, the most northern of the four historic Irish prov-inces, comprising nine of the island's thirty-two counties and amounting to roughly 8,950 square miles, just over a quarter of the island of Ireland's total area. Until the seventeenth century Ulster was isolated as a part of a Gaelic Ireland that had been more resis-tant than the three other Irish provinces to Norman and English rule since the twelfth century. The vast social engineering of the seventeenth century, however, resulted in the seizure of property and the removal of people on the basis of their religion, making the province a bastion of Protestant settlement and British influence. Plantation resulted in the seizure from Catholic natives of 5,600 square miles in Ulster, transforming the province with the arrival of English and Scottish settlers who differed in terms of religious affiliation (the English belonging to the established Anglican Church and the Scots Presbyterian) but had a common bond of 'Britishness', a term novel at that stage and one 'especially applied to those engaged in colonial endeavour'.[1]

But full 'British' control of Ulster was not achieved; while there was some assimilation and accommodation between these settlers and the Catholic natives, any possibility of permanent harmony was shattered by the Ulster rebellion of 1641, spearheaded by Catholics who retained land and status, with Ireland for the next ten years 'a theatre of war in the War of the Three Kingdoms; and for the ten years after that she found herself a laboratory for Cromwellian experiments'.[2] This included atrocities on a grand scale with the killing of soldiers, civilians and Catholic clergy. With the restoration of monarchy in 1660 there were hopes for a Catholic resurgence that were scuppered at the battles of the Boyne (1690) and Aughrim (1691), which confirmed Protestant dominance. Presbyterians were also excluded from the fruits of victory. But the Catholic question reignited in the late eighteenth century and rebellion in 1798 by a combination of radical Catholics and Protestants seeking the removal of English influence in Ireland stoked further enmities and fears about the stability of the Anglo-Irish connection. In response, the Act of Union was passed in 1800 creating the United Kingdom of Great Britain and Ireland and providing that Ireland be represented at Westminster by 100 MPs.

Over the course of the nineteenth century increasing Catholic and nationalist confidence and demands were manifest in southern Ireland; by 1861 just 8.9 per cent of the population of the three southern provinces was Protestant while the figure in Ulster was 49.5 per cent, a figure that steadily increased to 55.8 per cent by 1901.[3] The industrialisation of Belfast and the Lagan Valley in the nineteenth century also set it apart from a country that was overwhelmingly agrarian; there was consensus that Belfast as it thrived and expanded was more 'British', and that Ulster was 'different' from the rest of Ireland.[4]

By 1886 the British prime minister, William Gladstone, had decided home rule for Ireland was feasible and convenient from both the British and Irish perspectives; by then, iconic nationalist leader Charles Stewart Parnell had built a formidable Irish Parliamentary Party (IPP) demanding Irish self-government within the empire and was now a key player in British as well as Irish politics. Unionists, however, island wide, were determined to resist this in defence of unity of the UK, and so began a four-decade struggle that ended in partition. Gladstone did not succeed with his Home Rule bills of 1886 and 1893, but home rule demands continued. Irish Nationalist MPs, somewhat adrift after the death of Parnell in 1891 but reunified under the leadership of John Redmond in 1900, continued to remain a thorn in the side of the British political establishment and the IPP held the balance of power in Westminster in 1910. By 1912, following an alliance between the British Liberal Party and Irish nationalists against the wishes of Conservatives and unionists, and helped by the eradication of the House of Lords veto on legislation from the House of Commons, home rule was a distinct likelihood without any solution to unionist resistance, now being spearheaded by Dublin-born lawyer Edward Carson, leader of the Ulster Unionist Party from 1910. Prime Minister Herbert Asquith, lacking real conviction about the merits of home rule but in debt to the IPP for their support of reform of the House of Lords, duly introduced the third Home

Rule Bill in April 1912, declaring it would give Ireland ample scope for the development of its own 'national life' while binding Ireland to the empire through a sense of voluntary co-operation. This became the Home Rule Act in September 1914. Asquith, however, underestimated the gravity of the Ulster problem.

During this period the increasing 'Ulsterisation' of the unionist focus was hardened by the militancy of the Loyal Orange Institution (or the Orange Order), the Protestant defensive alliance with the greatest longevity, dating back to 1795 and now with a new lease of life. It was deemed pragmatic by unionists to defend the area where they were more numerous than to attempt to sustain an all-island opposition to Irish nationalist aspirations. Greater defiance included the signing of a covenant, a pact with God, in 1912, pledging to use 'all means necessary to defeat the present conspiracy to set up a Home Rule Parliament in Ireland' and the creation of an Ulster Volunteer Force in 1913 to resist by force of arms home rule being implemented. This was blatant rebellion, and it was tolerated by British authorities in a manner that did not extend to Irish nationalists pledged through their own Irish Volunteer organisation to fight for home rule's imposition. Leading Conservative politicians, including party leader Andrew Bonar Law, who had an Ulster Presbyterian background and who led opposition to the government from 1911 to 1915, backed the Ulster opposition to home rule, joining seventy other Conservative MPs at a unionist demonstration in Balmoral in 1912.

There were, as a result of this polarisation, two 'minority' issues in Ireland: the status of nationalists in Ulster and the position of unionists in Ireland as a whole, and religion was central to their politics.[5] The Irish Unionist Alliance in 1907 had stoked fears of Catholic domination in Ireland by insisting home rule would mean Rome rule: 'The people of Ulster are largely Protestant. They believe – and who are capable of judging better – that a home ruled Ireland would be an Ireland mainly dominated by the ideas of the Irish Roman Catholic hierarchy and clergy, who claim authority as much in temporal or secular affairs as they do in matters religious or spiritual.'[6] But it would be a mistake to see Ulster Protestant identity as axiomatically a British one; as historian Oliver MacDonagh saw it, Ulster for northern Protestants was 'more than a province, less than a state; it constituted at least a people'.[7] Many unionist activists came to see themselves as Ulster people, not Britons.[8]

Partition became a reality on the back of extraordinary upheavals in the decade after 1912, not least the First World War, during which over 200,000 Irishmen, unionist and nationalist, served in the British army. The implementation of home rule was postponed for the duration of the war without any solution to the Ulster crisis. In the spring of 1914 John Redmond reluctantly agreed to individual Ulster counties opting out of home rule for six years, a period rejected by Edward Carson who characterised it as 'a sentence of death with a stay of execution'.[9] The war effort was backed by Redmond and his constitutional nationalists as well as by Ulster unionists, who suffered catastrophic losses, in particular at the Battle of the Somme in July 1916. Overall, some 40,000 Irishmen lost their lives in the war.

The longer the war endured the more emboldened a minority of radical separatists in Ireland became, leading to the April 1916 Rising during which an Irish Republic was declared in Dublin, further increasing the ideological gulf between Ulster and the South. In its wake, Sinn Féin (meaning 'Ourselves') a political movement established in 1905, capitalised on the transformation in public opinion in southern Ireland after Britain executed the leaders of the rebellion and interned almost 2,000 suspected of involvement. Under the leadership of Éamon de Valera, a surviving commandant of the Easter Rising, and his deputy president,

Arthur Griffith, the original founder of Sinn Féin, the party triumphed in the 1918 general election and decimated the IPP. A war of independence between crown forces and the Irish Republican Army (which had evolved from the Irish Volunteer organisation) followed, while the Irish civil war raged from 1922 to 1923 as the Irish republican movement was ripped apart by the fallout from the signing of the Anglo-Irish Treaty between Irish republicans and the British government in December 1921 that created a free state in southern Ireland, a dominion of the British empire.

Crucially, the British government did not negotiate with Irish republicans until it had first addressed the Ulster question. Partition had been suggested as a solution to the home rule problem by Liberal MP Thomas Agar-Robartes in June 1912, the idea being centred on the exclusion from home rule of four Ulster counties: Antrim, Down, Armagh and Derry. Agar-Robartes received support from some unionists, essentially because of their distrust not only of Irish nationalists but also of southern unionists and British Liberals and Tories; partition was ultimately about the triumph of localism and all the narrow-mindedness that went with that. While Edward Carson, who led the Unionist parliamentarians until 1921, was of the view that Ireland was an indivisible unit, by 1916 he and the Ulster Unionist Council, the umbrella body designed from 1905 to unite various unionist organisations and bind Unionist MPs to their constituents, accepted the principle of the exclusion of six counties of Ulster (Fermanagh and Tyrone added to the original four above), because, if full union could not be maintained, this was deemed the best alternative.

That year was also a crucial one for nationalists in Ulster, as their 1916 conference in Belfast sparked a stinging conflict between home rulers and Sinn Féin. Set up by Joe Devlin, a key organiser and IPP MP for Ulster nationalists, and addressed by John Redmond, the Ulster Nationalist Conference voted to accept a

proposal for 'temporary' exclusion of the six north-eastern counties as the price for the early implementation of home rule. But
there was a clear geographical divide; delegates from Fermanagh,
Tyrone and Derry City – mid Ulster – voted firmly against this
proposal.[10]

Carson was still privately open to the idea of an alternative
and in March 1917 prepared a plan to tempt Ulster into devolved
Irish government, whereby Ulster would be left out of home rule
but an all-Ireland council with representatives of a home rule Parliament and Ulster MPs at Westminster would consider legislative proposals for the whole of Ireland and 'frame a procedure by
which if agreement was reached they could be enacted simultaneously in Dublin and the excluded counties'.[11] The British government was open to this and Carson was willing to try to sell it to
his party, but it was shelved in favour of the Irish Convention that
lasted from July 1917 to April 1918. This was a doomed attempt to
negotiate a settlement between nationalists and unionists devised
by David Lloyd George (British prime minister since December
1916), largely for the optics and as a response to American pressure. Lloyd George, and before him Herbert Asquith, were more
preoccupied with how the Irish question would affect their own
party and British politics than its potential impact on Ireland,
which was too often a pawn in the game of their career advance-
ment.[12] There were serious consequences for Ireland as a result.

The triumph of Sinn Féin in the December 1918 election,
winning seventy-three seats on an abstention from Westminster
platform and with a demand for a thirty-two-county Irish republic, further polarised Ireland. With the First World War now over,
the Irish question had to be confronted once more; unionists
were helped by the presence at cabinet of Walter Long who had
led the Irish Unionists between 1906 and 1910 and now headed
the cabinet committee on Irish affairs. Details of a partition plan

were gradually worked out and though there was some sympathy at government level for the nationalists, 'the only Irishmen to be consulted were [James] Craig and his associates'.[13] Craig, a principal architect of opposition to the third Home Rule Bill, was also serving in a government position, and took over from the declining Carson as Ulster Unionist leader in early 1921.

But it was Walter Long who, from 1919, had most influence over the British cabinet, and what was decided under his direction was that it was not enough to repeal the 1914 Home Rule Act; what was needed was unity of empire (therefore no Irish republic), no coercion of Ulster, a Parliament for southern Ireland, another for Ulster if it so chose, and a Council of Ireland 'as a means of enabling Ireland to work out her own salvation'.[14] It was envisaged that the new Act would ultimately lead to Irish unity, but if the two parliaments could not agree to come together they could stay in isolation; there would be no forcing of Ulster to join the South but neither was there an assumption Ulster would remain a fully integrated part of the UK. It was clear that partition was being imposed by Britain, but, as Ronan Fanning characterised it, 'the ending of partition would be a matter for the Irish'.[15]

What was attractive for Long's committee was the possibility of 'the complete withdrawal of British rule from all of Ireland in all matters not especially reserved' as its presence had been the 'tap root of the Irish difficulty'.[16] While the British preference was for a nine-county Ulster solution, Craig preferred six because Antrim, Armagh, Down, Fermanagh, Derry and Tyrone comprised the largest area where there was a 'decisive Protestant majority in which unionist power could be guaranteed in perpetuity'.[17] Ronan Fanning, in dissecting cabinet discussions of 1919, notes that 'Ulstercentricity' was paramount; it was known that Sinn Féin would reject these proposals; as Lord Chancellor F. E. Smith saw it, the Bill was about, not coming to terms with Irish republicans but the 'strengthening of our tactical position before the world'.

But there was also no doubt that Long's initiative, with the backing of Lloyd George (keen to placate US opinion), was also about some dilution of the Union; as Carson commented acidly in December 1919 about the government's attitude towards unionists, 'you still want to kick them out as if they were of no use'. The cabinet had been told the previous month that Ulster unionists would not be 'on the same footing as citizens of Great Britain' but 'subject to a different *régime*'.[18]

What transpired was the Government of Ireland Act, sometimes known as the Partition Act; it provided for separate parliaments for six Ulster counties and southern Ireland and, though rejected by Sinn Féin, it provided the constitutional framework for the creation of Northern Ireland, of which James Craig became the first prime minister in 1921. The Act was also a reflection of the growing determination of British politicians to get the Irish question off its tables; the Tories no longer needed or wanted to rally around Unionists, and Liberals were no longer courting Irish votes.[19] As Philip Kerr, an adviser to David Lloyd George wrote, 'It would at least accomplish two essential things: it would take Ulster out of the Irish question which it had blocked for a generation and it would take Ireland out of English party controversies.'[20] That was the privately acknowledged reality and did not suggest any sense of an Ulster unionism being valued or cherished by the British political establishment (thirteen Irish MPs would continue to represent Northern Ireland at Westminster). Northern Ireland, with a population of roughly 1.6 million, 430,000 of whom were Catholic, was, and remained, an expensive nuisance; at the outset of its existence, four-fifths of the Belfast government's revenue came from London.[21]

What the new border meant in physical terms was that

county lines that had been established in the sixteenth and seventeenth centuries were adhered to regardless of what they crossed; county boundaries had often run along rivers, which later attracted urban settlements, so the hinterlands of a number of towns were now split and even individual farms and houses were divided by the border. Quite simply, the partition line was arbitrary; using county borders also meant that many nationalists and unionists were left on the 'wrong' side and it inevitably ruptured communities. Clerical administrative units would also cross the border and the Catholic primate of *all* Ireland was and remained based in Armagh.

The new border's physical manifestations were ridiculous. T. W. Freeman, a pioneer of geographical studies in Ireland, published his book *Ireland* in 1950 and noted 'no clear boundary exists, for County Armagh meets Monaghan in what is generally a farmed landscape'.[22] Or, as economic historian D. S. Johnson later put it, 'like the equator, the border is an invisible line'.[23] As was apparent from the first Ordnance Survey of Northern Ireland in 1938 'it was blessed with one of the densest rural road networks, in terms of population, if not area, in western Europe. No less than 180 roads crossed the border and in some thirty-five to forty instances they defined it, with the frontier lying in the middle and a crossing point every mile.'[24] But only a fraction of these – sixteen – were 'approved' border roads from the 1920s. In one case that came to light in 1937 a house in Fermanagh was divided by the border, and the Catholic Registration Association unsuccessfully attempted to disenfranchise four Protestants on the grounds that they slept in a part of the house that was in a 'foreign' country (the Irish Free State), though the kitchen and sitting room were in Northern Ireland.[25]

Was this partition a British construct? That was certainly the central plank of subsequent nationalist narratives; as David

O'Neill saw it in *The Partition of Ireland* (1949), it was an 'outrage' that was 'committed upon Ireland' by British politicians 'in pursuant of their own party politics'.[26] Denis Gwynn argued in his history of partition the following year (his father Stephen had been an MP and strong defender of John Redmond), 'Lloyd George's record in the whole story of Partition shows a completely opportunist attitude.'[27] Frank Gallagher's *The Indivisible Island* (1957) continued this focus, with Ireland depicted as a pawn in a British party game and a victim of a powerful empire.

That was only part of the story, however, and partition was born with the assistance of Irish midwives also, unionist and nationalist. Despite Craig's assertion that it was a 'supreme sacrifice' for unionists, who were now abandoning southern unionists (in 1911 there were 327,179 Protestants in southern Ireland, where the overall population was about 2.8 million), as far back as 1910 he had asserted 'perhaps we should change our tactics ... it strikes me that a great deal of the energy and money would be much better expended by just letting Ulster take her own firm stand'.[28] His brother Charles Craig, Unionist MP for South Antrim, offered another reason by telling the House of Commons in March 1920 that unionists now wanted their own Parliament because a 'profound mistrust of the Labour party and of the Liberal leader Asquith made Unionists believe that if either of those parties were in power again, unionist chances of remaining in the UK would be very small'.[29]

Fred Crawford, a key figure on the secret military committee of the Ulster Unionist Council, asserted, 'I consider that by voting for the six counties I have kept my [1912] covenant both in spirit and letter. My objective in signing the Covenant was to keep Ulster Protestant, and free from any possibility of becoming a part of a Home Rule Ireland with one Parliament in Dublin.'[30] And there, laid bare, was the sectarian reality; to 'keep Ulster

Protestant' was the bedrock on which Ulster unionists built their acceptance of partition. Of fifty-two MPs in the Northern Ireland House of Commons elected in May 1921, forty were unionist and nationalists and republicans divided the remaining spoils, establishing the pattern that endured. Sectarian violence also marred the state's birth; between July 1920 and July 1922 there were 557 people killed; 303 Catholics, 172 Protestants and 82 members of the police and British forces.[31]

The 1920 Bill did not solve the Irish crisis; Sinn Féin rejected it, and was by then conducting a political war of independence and building a republican state to try to supplant the British administration in Ireland while the IRA waged a parallel military war of independence. The cessation of violence in July 1921 was followed by negotiations between Sinn Féin and the government led by David Lloyd George, which led to a new chapter in the Irish border saga. Éamon de Valera refused to lead the Irish delegation and remained in Dublin while Arthur Griffith embraced the task. Lloyd George was seen by some as one who betrayed his sympathy for the South in the face of what Griffith, in London from October to December 1921, referred to bitingly as the 'cloven hoof of Ulster's sordidness'.[32] Griffith was ultimately to become impaled on the Ulster cross, though he also hammered more nails into it than were necessary.

The British were determined to avoid a collapse of the talks over 'Ulster', where, as Lloyd George admitted, they had a weaker case (owing to the political and economic consequences of dividing such a small country) than on the question of Ireland staying in the empire. In September 1921 Lloyd George had been privately adamant that, while British soldiers might die for the throne and empire, 'I do not know who will die for Tyrone and Fermanagh. The feeling here is not so strong as in 1913/14. Lots feel a bit annoyed about Ulster, think them unreasonable, narrow.'[33] The

Irish delegates insisted on local plebiscites as a way to determine the contested border but were prepared to allow Northern Ireland to retain its existing territory, Parliament and government if the Unionists would agree to these being subordinate to Dublin and not London, or what was regarded as 'essential unity', which the Unionists emphatically rejected.

Lloyd George found James Craig 'reasonable' in November 1921; 'he discussed conditions under which an all-Ireland Parliament would function ... but when he came again on Monday afternoon he had changed; under no circumstances could Ulster look at an all-Ireland Parliament', to which Lloyd George responded, 'we will not force. A Boundary Commission ... is a defensible position.'[34] While Craig refused to be blinkered by the charm and chancing of the prime minister, Lloyd George pushed this Boundary Commission idea to determine the Irish border, a commission that would supposedly examine the distribution of population along the border of the six counties to ascertain which side they should be or wished to be on; the cabinet had been told in late 1919 that James Craig had privately suggested such an initiative.[35]

Griffith responded by insisting the division of Ireland was 'unnatural' ('what you have done is as if some few counties in England had been separated from the rest') and he maintained naïvely that if the Ulster Unionists did not have the backing of the British government 'we could settle the Ulster question'. He also suggested unionists had their own distinctive identity, remarking that there were two ways to annoy a working-class unionist: 'one was to speak respectfully of the Pope, the other was to call him an Englishman'. Lloyd George was also happy to elaborate on the unionists' psychology: 'They are a pugnacious people with a touch of the Scotch about them which is a very stubborn race ... we are only behind them to the extent that we cannot allow civil war to take place at our doors which will embroil our own people ... there is nothing we would like better than that they should unite with you ... we stand neutral.'[36] This highly qualified commitment to Ulster's unionists remained relevant in subsequent decades.

Griffith, however, was ultimately and too easily steamrollered by Lloyd George into a private agreement that he would not repudiate a plan for a Boundary Commission and compromise Lloyd George's position with his Conservative and unionist critics. The crucial point was that Griffith was encouraged to believe that the Boundary Commission would transfer significant areas of Northern Ireland to the proposed new dominion in the twenty-six counties of southern Ireland, what became the Irish Free State and after 1949 the Irish Republic. As Griffith saw it, according to Lloyd George's secretary, Tom Jones, 'we would prefer a plebiscite but in essentials a Boundary Commission is very much the same.'[37] It certainly was not.

There were a number of Lloyd Georges on display during these talks; he gave various impressions as to what he would do about Ulster obduracy, including 'apparently' threatening to resign. It is ironic indeed that it was James Craig who, when he met Éamon de Valera in 1921, warned him never to meet Lloyd George alone as he would give any account of the interview that suited him.[38] Edward Carson also claimed (in 1924) that he had received a letter from Lloyd George in 1920 assuring him of 'permanent' exclusion of the six counties from any settlement with nationalist Ireland. But when writing to Craig in November 1921 Lloyd George had decried the idea of a partition that would involve 'cutting the natural circuits of commercial activity', and said that 'when such frontiers are established they harden into permanence'. A few weeks later he suggested that if Northern Ireland chose not to integrate into the new southern Free State, 'we should feel unable to defend the present boundary, which must be subject to revision on one side and the other by a Boundary

Commission'. Less than two weeks later he insisted in the House of Commons that while he was 'against the coercion of Ulster, I do not believe in Ulster coercing other units. Apart from that, would it be an advantage to Ulster? There is no doubt it would give her trouble.'[39]

The diaries of Tom Jones also highlight the considerable contempt of some British politicians towards Ireland throughout this process. Andrew Bonar Law told Jones he had come to the conclusion 'that the Irish were an inferior race'. Jones suggested euphemistically 'there was an incapacity to see Ireland clearly' but that 'all this changed in 1921'.[40] Lloyd George was consistent in his contention 'we cannot coerce Ulster' but also made the revealing comment that 'The Britisher would pay a good deal for a quiet life'; the imperative was to get the Irish question away from Downing Street and there was a constant irritation about Ulster and little warmth towards its champions. Former prime minister Arthur Balfour recognised the unionist case for shaping its own destiny 'in spite of her bigotry'.[41]

Tom Jones saw Griffith alone in November 1921 and suggested that if Sinn Féin co-operated with Lloyd George's strategy, 'we might have Ulster in before many months had passed'.[42] The following month, the day before the Anglo-Irish Treaty was signed, creating the new southern Irish dominion, a panicked Griffith asked, 'cannot you ... get from Craig a conditional recognition, however shadowy, of Irish national unity?' in return for the acceptance of allegiance to the empire by an Irish Free State. But the desperate plea was in vain; instead, the Boundary Commission proposal was incorporated into Article 12 of the Anglo-Irish Treaty; it stipulated that if Northern Ireland opted not to join the Irish Free State, as was its right under the treaty, the Boundary Commission would determine the border 'in accordance with the wishes of the inhabitants, so far as may be compatible with economic and geographic conditions'. The impression created of such a commission during the talks, as recorded by Tom Jones was that it would involve 'so cutting down Ulster that she would be forced in from economic necessity'.[43] Job done, Lloyd George boasted 'we've got rid' of the Irish question while maintaining in relation to Ulster, 'we have emancipated her'.[44]

Both Arthur Griffith and Michael Collins (who as director of intelligence of the IRA and Sinn Féin minister for finance had played a pivotal role in the war of independence before becoming part of the Irish negotiating team) expected 'the Boundary Commission to carve out large chunks of Craig's jurisdiction within the year' if Craig did not agree to join the Irish Free State. As Collins put it, 'any kind of even temporary partition is distasteful to me. We may reduce the North East area [as Sinn Féin referred to it] to such limits that it cannot exist without us, and that it will be forced in. But there would be such rancour.'[45] That was the problem and there it was left hanging; Collins had an idea that he could do business with Craig and therefore eliminate 'English interference'. The problem, however, was that there was an alternative southern Irish nationalist narrative about the border, neatly encapsulated in de Valera's logic; partition had been imposed by the British government and needed to be undone by a British government.

Craig, meanwhile, spoke of the betrayal of unionists because of the inclusion of the Boundary Commission clause and wrote to Lloyd George in mid December reminding him that he had promised on 25 November that 'the rights of Ulster will be in no way sacrificed or compromised' and that 'at our meeting on December 9 you complained that it was only intended to make a slight readjustment of our boundary line, so as to bring in to Northern Ireland loyalists who are now just outside our area and to transfer correspondingly an equivalent number of those having

Sinn Féin sympathies to the area of the Irish Free State'. But since then, members of government had 'given encouragement to those endeavouring to read into it a different interpretation'. Craig also objected to automatic inclusion in the proposed Irish Free State as provided by the treaty, even if it came with the right of unionists to then opt out, which they did, exactly one year after the treaty was signed.[46] Despite his crocodile tears, what Craig had – a partitioned Ireland and a unionist state of Northern Ireland – he was determined, and very well placed, to hold.

The treaty divided Sinn Féin and ultimately led to a civil war, not over the Boundary Commission but over a contested oath of allegiance to the British crown to be taken by Irish parliamentarians; indeed, the Boundary Commission idea was not even a central part of the acrimonious Treaty Debates in December 1921 and January 1922 in Dublin. This highlighted the broad belief that the Commission would 'deliver' for the South, but also the failure to engage with the reality of the unionist mentality, long an Achilles heel of Irish nationalism.

At the same time, assertions of British neutrality on the Irish question were far fetched; it is striking, for example, that during the bloody birth of Northern Ireland and afterwards, London deliberately turned a blind eye to 'Ulster Loyalists' engaged in killing, and monitoring of them remained a deliberate gap in British intelligence. Those 'pugnacious' veterans of the Ulster rebellion of 1913/14 were rewarded with unchecked control of law and order and 'myopia about Loyalist violence persisted for decades', the British preference being to monitor Irish republicans.[47] The British government, despite some reservations, did not shirk from providing plentiful supplies and arms to Northern Ireland for its defence and this ensured Northern Ireland was 'inured to political realities'.[48] There is little doubt that Winston Churchill, secretary of state for the colonies in 1921, was opposed to forcing Unionists into a united Ireland, and would have been 'delighted if they had been successfully persuaded', but when he was chancellor of the exchequer in the 1920s he was effectively responsible for under-pinning the new state by breaking the British treasury consensus that Northern Ireland should pay for its own upkeep.

But there was also the reality, suggested by Lord Salisbury, a senior Conservative, that the average English voter had 'little interest in, and less understanding of, Irish affairs'.[49] Lillian Spender, the wife of Wilfred Bliss Spender, a militant veteran of the UVF and decorated British army soldier who became cabinet secretary in Northern Ireland in 1921, recorded the observations of a friend a week after the Treaty was signed: 'England doesn't want us.'[50] Northern nationalists, now truly abandoned, felt the same about Dublin. Historian Charles Townshend has also reminded, with biting accuracy, of leading politicians who were 'thoroughly English in seeing Ireland as a confounded nuisance'; the British government 'took little interest' in Ireland and 'Ministers respon-sible for Ireland, usually second-rankers, had difficulty in find-ing an audience for their views'. There would be no going back to the days when it dominated, and ignorance too often replaced absorption. But it was a myth to suggest, as A. J. P. Taylor did in 1965, that Lloyd-George had 'conjured' the Irish problem 'out of existence'.[51] Instead, the problem was shelved.

When Ulster was useful for British politicians for their own ends they exploited the connection, but they would eventually get to the stage where, in the words of Austen Chamberlain in 1924, they would do their utmost to prevent it being 'a fatal influence on British politics'.[52] More crude, but no less accurate, and an indica-tion of the difficulty of commanding attention, were the words of Northern Ireland labour activist and East Belfast MP Jack Beattie in the 1920s when he insisted Northern Ireland should not remain the 'moth-eaten tail of the British lion'.[53] British Labour opinion on Ireland had been broadly anti-partitionist; its 1918 conference had advocated 'self-determination in all exclusively Irish affairs', but that policy oscillated. Its championing of 'free and absolute self-determination' and opposition to the partitionist nature of the Government of Ireland Bill of 1920 (J. R. Clynes, briefly Labour Party leader from 1921 to 1922, insisted there should be 'one parliament speaking for one united Ireland') moved by 1921 to an insistence on the protection of minorities and ultimately an acceptance of the treaty. Its opposition to partition was only steadfast 'until the proposal became a reality'.[54] Labour shared the sigh of relief, it seemed, that the treaty generated in the wider British political context. Such an attitude was cemented by power, which Labour achieved in January 1924: George Lansbury, future party leader, declared in 1925 that Ireland is 'a question which is practically settled today'.[55]

But it was not a settled issue in Ireland. Before his untimely death during the Irish civil war in 1922, Michael Collins had sought desperately to reconcile his republican beliefs with the compromise that was the Anglo-Irish Treaty. In the first half of 1922 he met with James Craig to discuss what became 'pacts' in relation to security, the reinstatement of expelled Catholic workers and the ending of a republican boycott of produce from Northern Ireland, but such agreements also bestowed a certain recognition of the state of Northern Ireland. In parallel, Collins also secretly gave the nod for a northern offensive by the IRA to try to undermine Craig's government and to find a unifying focus for the republican paramilitary movement. It was a dismal failure, and its hollowness was further underlined in October 1922, when a deputation including priests, solicitors and local councillors from Northern Ireland arrived in Dublin to the provisional government of the Irish Free State looking for funds to counteract unionist propaganda.

They got short shrift from Kevin O'Higgins, the new minister for home affairs: 'We have no other policy for the North East than we have for any other part of Ireland and that is the Treaty policy.' He suggested that what northern nationalists needed was not just funds but 'a great deal of strenuous voluntary work – just the same sort of strenuous work that brought the national position to the stage it has reached'.[56] The washing of southern hands could hardly have been more apparent; O'Higgins claimed the real problem was the lack of cohesion on the part of nationalists. An interned teacher in Belfast in January 1923 wrote to the Free State's minister for education using words that proved accurate indeed: 'the bitter part is the reflection that when I do get out I shall probably be forgotten'.[57]

2

An Entrenched Partition

How the Catholic minority in Northern Ireland fared in the 1920s and beyond has been deftly delineated by Eamon Phoenix in *Northern Nationalism* (1994); those who, in the words of Ulster nationalist MP Joe Devlin, who led nationalists in and out of Northern Ireland's Stormont Parliament in Belfast from the mid 1920s to the mid 1930s, were kept 'as one third of the population as if they were pariahs'. Devlin faced a great quandary in trying to unite nationalists; there was still a divide between those in the border regions and those further east, and nationalists were also split on the extent to which for practical and economic reasons they should work with the state rather than seek to resist or undermine it. In all this they got precious little help from Dublin governments, who spoke of non-recognition of Northern Ireland but did little beyond this, and Ulster nationalists regarded the reaction of the south as a 'callous betrayal'.[1]

During the disturbances in Northern Ireland from 1920 to 1922, 7,500 Catholic workers were expelled, almost one-third of the entire Catholic workforce, and many were forced into slum housing. Over a hundred people died in Belfast alone in 1921, rising to nearly 300 in 1922, as a result of sectarian violence. Partition also increased segregation, and from 1911 to 1926, the 'primary determinant of working-class residence patterns was ethnic violence and the fear of it'.[2] Northern Ireland Catholics were two and a half times more likely to be unemployed than their Protestant counterparts, and in the newly created civil service of Northern Ireland the proportion of senior-grade posts occupied by Catholics in 1927 was no more than 6 per cent.[3]

Neither did the abolition of proportional representation for parliamentary elections in 1929 help northern nationalists; they ended up mixing abstention and participation (unionists ignored them in Parliament) all the while experiencing an icy chill from Dublin. They were also far too reliant on the Catholic Church in Northern Ireland and before the formation of a new Nationalist Party in 1928 they consulted the bishops, desiring to 'solicit their approval'.[4] The Catholic Church in Northern Ireland suited itself; Cardinal MacRory, Catholic primate of all Ireland, urged non-recognition of the state but diluted that because he wanted to control Catholic education, all the while denouncing partition and maintaining that the various Protestant churches were 'not even part of the Church of Christ'.[5]

The fate of unionists left on the 'wrong' side of the border was also problematic. Norma MacMaster's novel *Silence Under a Stone* (2017), spanning the 1920s to the 1980s, focuses on Harriet and Tom Campbell, strict Presbyterians living just south of the border in the 1920s, feeling marooned on the wrong side and completely suffocated by an authoritarian Catholicism. Rome 'truly haunted our lives', Harriet asserts, but they are also hemmed in by their own introverted evangelical world.[6] The *Church of Ireland Gazette* in January 1922 declared that, for southern loyalists:

> Ireland is their country. Thousands of them will never leave its shores; they are determined to make the best of things,

continuing in the future, as in the past, to work for the good of their native land ... in accepting the new scheme of things without demur, the loyalists of the South and West are taking a considerable risk. They are committing themselves and their children to the unknown, and their only guarantee is the instinctive faith in the justice of their fellow-countrymen.[7]

In September 1922, however, the Church of Ireland Bishop of Kilmore told the annual Diocesan Synod that 'the Church had suffered severely' and that emigration from the south and west had been 'calamitous'.

Between 1911 and 1926, the decline in the southern Irish Protestant population was 33 per cent (in contrast to only 2 per cent for Catholics). This thinning out did not begin with partition; it had begun with the land war of the nineteenth century as tenants sought ownership of land and to break the power of the landlord class.[8]

Other departures were due to military service and the effects of the First World War, but there was still 'the inevitable conclusion that a significant proportion of the overall decline was due to involuntary migration, recently assessed at about 39,000 from the South ... this exodus constitutes about 37 per cent of the Protestant population decline between 1911 and 1926'.[9]

There was undoubtedly trauma on a serious scale due to revolutionary violence, but

ultimately, the majority of Protestants remained in Ireland and ... the political question was reasonably sensitive to their position. At the outset, at least, they were over represented in both the Senate and the Dáil [the Irish Free State's Parliament]; they retained ownership of a disproportionate share of land in the state and retained a dominant position in industry, finance and the professions.[10]

Protestants had comprised about 10 per cent of the population in the South in the early twentieth century, reduced to 7 per cent by 1926, yet still produced 40 per cent of lawyers and over 50 per cent of bankers, and over a quarter of large farms were still in Protestant ownership. Clearly, many were not 'wounded beasts' that tended to 'curl into a ball'.[11] Many shared the conservatism of their Catholic counterparts when it came to 'family values' and matters such as divorce and abortion, though issues like hospital control developed tensions. They also had their newspaper, the *Irish Times*, which 'helped to supply an essential narrative of continuity, easing the unionists into a tolerance – albeit often begrudgingly – of the new Ireland'.[12] By the 1930s, Protestants had ceased to be an organised political force in their own right.[13] Yet their sense of alienation was 'modified and mediated' through separate social and commercial spheres; southern Protestants had their own schools, clubs and societies and patronised Protestant banks and businesses.[14]

There have been revealing studies of individual border counties and the plight of the minorities within them, including Monaghan Protestants who had from 1912 been an integral part of the unionist movement. One of the three TDs elected for the county was usually a Protestant, and Terry Dooley has noted that 'Protestants living under Dublin rule had less to grieve about than Catholics in neighbouring South Fermanagh, South Tyrone and Armagh who were living under Belfast Rule'.[15] Brian Hughes, in his examination of Cavan Protestants (a surviving record of Protestant migration into Fermanagh includes 145 Protestant persons or families who left Cavan between 1920 and 1925) concludes, 'For most, assimilation came easily, if not always graciously, and residues of old loyalties remained ... in a wider European context, it was a relatively peaceful transition.'[16] This is a point that has been elaborated on by other historians in relation to both sides of the Irish border, Gearóid Ó Tuathaigh pointing out that, given the fate of European minorities in the 1920s, 'it is reasonable to ask whether the fate of Irish minorities under partition was the worst that could have befallen them'.[17]

Many in Donegal, Catholics and Protestants, felt a particular isolation, left abandoned by both North and South and their grievances – the erosion of railways, poor land, inadequate healthcare, prosperous Eastern Donegal farmers who took their business north – endured. Donegal was often seen as a place apart and went defiantly its own way, being on the 'outer edge of Ulster'. Fánaid, for example, the peninsula forming the western shore of Lough Swilly and jutting into the Atlantic from the north-west coast with jagged cliffs, low hills and lake-dotted bog, had long been regarded by the more prosperous as 'beyond the frontier of respectability'. Its inhabitants in the nineteenth century were seen as a 'rude people' and a 'lawless and truculent body' with a 'spirit of insubordination'. It was denuded by famine and emigration and shorn of 'vital elements of cultural reproduction': its population of 10,344 in 1841 was reduced to just 5,778 in 1891 and merely 2,846 in 1961.[18]

That the border had profound economic consequences became quickly apparent in the 1920s and it inevitably bred smuggling, made even more attractive by the decisions taken on fiscal policy in the early 1920s. In April 1923 a new customs tariff imposed by the Irish Free State came into existence between North and South; it was referred to by an *Irish Times* reporter as

> our new fiscal independence ... at present the only things that are not dearer in Dublin than in Belfast are the

dutiable articles, the transference of which from one territory to the other accordingly offers no advantage. By and
by, when our tobacco and cigarettes have begun to cost the
extra threepence in the shilling and the local table water
merchants have started a Ginger Beer Trust, smuggling will
begin to be worth while.[19]

This was in the dying days of the Irish civil war, with predictions
that the Irish Free State government would carry a deficit of
£20 million, in contrast to a Northern Ireland that could balance
its books, but it remained to be seen if raising revenue through
tariffs would be undermined by loss of trade.[20]

There was also the still-unresolved politics of the border,
wrapped up in the Boundary Commission dilemma. The British
Labour Party had been cautious about the Commission, which
began work in November 1924 and its parliamentary party,
according to minutes of its executive in May 1924, was hostile to
the idea of 'reopening the whole Irish question'. It was far more
concerned with domestic issues and its left wing wasn't exactly
enamoured at the Conservative Irish Free State; historian George
Boyce suggested that Labour's pragmatic tepidity over time meant
'it had no Irish past to live down or live up to'.[21]

In contrast, the Irish Free State government led by Prime Minister William T. Cosgrave and his Cumann na nGaedheal Party
from 1922 to 1932 (their republican opponents abstained from the
Dáil until 1927) had to contend with the weight of expectation
that the Commission would redraw the border. For all its wariness
about embracing northern nationalists and its understandable
preoccupation with civil war and its aftermath, perilous finances
and instability in the army, the Irish government had not buried
its head regarding the Commission. Nor was there inevitability
about the outcome of its deliberations.

Senior Irish officials who were involved in the North-Eastern Boundary Bureau, established by the Irish Free State government to make the case for revision of the border through plebiscites, did considerable homework, though ultimately the Commission refused to consider its work, which amounted to some fifty-six boxes of files. Kevin O'Shiel, barrister and assistant legal adviser to the Irish Free State government and a native of Omagh in Tyrone, was appointed director of the Boundary Bureau in October 1922 and tasked with researching and compiling relevant data; his endeavours included travelling to Geneva to examine material from other boundary commissions at the League of Nations archives.

From the outset O'Shiel, who had coined the phrase 'a policy of peaceful do-nothingness' in preference to violent provocation of Northern Ireland during the civil war, was adamant about the need for efforts to centre on publicity and propaganda: 'we cannot underestimate the advantages of a judiciously arranged and timely press campaign ... in the two most recent European examples of partition – Silesia [between Germany and Poland] and Schleswig-Holsten [between Germany and Denmark] – an enormous literary propaganda was carried on throughout Europe by the various partisans'. For the League of Nations, the first significant border test involving the major Allied powers was Upper Silesia. The Allies had failed to define a boundary for the region based on the plebiscite results of 20 March 1921. A boundary determination was complicated, particularly in the prized area of the industrial triangle; most cities voted for Germany, while the surrounding areas voted for Poland. But the real complication was English and French inability to forgo their vested interests and establish a viable boundary that recognised both the wishes of the inhabitants and the 'geographic and economic conditions of the locality' as stipulated in the Treaty of Versailles. Likewise, the

Irish Boundary Commission, as seen earlier, was also supposed to consider a border 'in accordance with the wishes of the inhabitants, so far as may be compatible with economic and geographic conditions'.

O'Shiel's view of propaganda was that it would do much to 'influence world opinion'.[22] This might seem like naïve grandstanding, but there was more to it than that. In similar vein, like many of his contemporaries in 1922, George Gavan Duffy, briefly minister for external affairs in 1922, articulated what he felt were the opportunities for a small nation at that time. The new state, he asserted in a private letter, 'will bring into a tired world a freshness of vision, coupled with a directness and a tenacity of purpose that will gradually make her an active factor in the redemption of Europe'. He concluded defiantly that the new state would 'rapidly prove itself justly entitled to be called the first of the small nations'.[23]

O'Shiel sought to suffuse his memoranda on the border with similar defiance and optimism and the idea that the 'organised force of public opinion' would be the decisive factor in determining whether the Commission 'will lean towards our side of the case or the pro-Partition side'.[24] He also referred, in what might have been news to them, to 'our people in the six-county area'. The use of that description, 'six-county area' persisted for decades, in order to deny Northern Ireland recognition as a legitimate state. By the following year, a month after the end of the civil war, O'Shiel felt the time was ripe for renewed vigour on the border question and noted that the late Michael Collins had often remarked 'the Boundary Commission will settle nothing'. What was needed, argued O'Shiel, was to secure a national union, which would initially be likely to take some federal form, acknowledging 'there are sufficient differences to justify an autonomous parliament in that corner of Ireland'. O'Shiel also frequently referred to the 'die hard' and 'vehement' pro-Ulster enthusiasm of some Tories.[25]

More striking was O'Shiel's unfettered declaration that the promised land was in sight and clearly he practised what he preached in terms of the importance of propaganda: the government that achieved national unity 'will live in history as the government that performed the greatest piece of initial statesmanship in Ireland and laid the most solid and enduring foundations for peace. It is my belief that this immortal achievement is within the grasp of the present government.'[26] This was an extraordinary overstatement, but it is a reminder of a belief or hope that the Commission would deliver for the South. The following year, however, the North-Eastern Boundary Bureau was more sober: 'We are entirely in the dark as to how the Commission will result and its finding may prove much less favourable than most of us imagine.'[27]

There was speculation that the Irish Free State would get part of South Down and Fermanagh and that Northern Ireland would get part of Donegal adjacent to Derry. Two bleak likelihoods were apparent: there would still be many nationalists left in Northern Ireland and 'it is most improbable that it will so reduce the Northern area as to compel union'. Reality was dawning in other ways: 'It is a very different thing to draw a boundary in Upper Silesia between Germany and Poland which are to remain separate states and to draw it between the two parts of a country which we hope will eventually be one. The way the present business is conducted may mean the difference between union in 5 years or in a hundred.' The solution was deemed to lie in an offer of 'some system of joint government, giving an opportunity of advance to fuller union later'.[28]

There were other wider contexts that were relevant to the Irish Boundary Commission and the settling of borders. Margaret O'Callaghan points out that there was no 'stable British line' during this period about these issues due to changes of British government and the wider imperial and emerging commonwealth story.[29] It is noteworthy that partition in Ireland 'was the first major partition in which a British cabinet participated in territory which it had formerly controlled, but it provided a precedent for later partitions', including India and Palestine.[30] Religious differences were germane to these partitions along with a British government propensity to play one side against the other: Hindus and Muslims, Jews and Arabs ('Like the Ulster Protestants the Jews, too, were a settler community, of much more recent origin but with ancient connections with the area') and Catholics and Protestants. Destruction of lives and property preceded all these partitions; constitutionalists suffered marginalisation and there was little reconciliation to new boundaries.[31]

Palestine and Ireland also highlighted the difficulties of attempting to divide comparatively small units and the use of ambiguous language open to different interpretations. The Balfour Declaration of 1917, for example, averred that the British government 'views with favour the establishment of a national home for the Jewish people', subject to nothing being done 'which would prejudice the civil and religious rights of existing non-Jewish communities' in Palestine. Not only was this difficult to decipher, it was also, it seemed, irreconcilable with the assertion of the high commissioner in Cairo, Sir Henry McMahon, a few years previously when he said that Britain was prepared to 'recognise and support the independence of the Arabs'. The Irish Boundary Commission's wording about compatibility with economic and geographic conditions was also vague.

When Britain considered the partition of Palestine in the late 1930s 'the area allotted to the Jewish state contained 295,000 Arabs compared with 305,000 Jews. It was the same picture as in Tyrone, Fermanagh and the central Punjab.' These partitions did not serve as successful solutions; what was different about

Ireland in comparison with India and Palestine was that there was no large-scale population movement as a result of the partition.[32] Crucially, these partitions also 'largely ignored economics', even though the economic arguments were held to be important considerations against partition and were enunciated by Lloyd George in the Irish context, while Mohammed Ali Jinnah of the Muslim League was bitterly opposed to a Pakistan that would break the economic unity of Bengal and the Punjab.

It was also pertinent that many in British politics would have preferred unity in Ireland while the partition of Palestine was 'bitterly opposed' by the British Foreign Office, but David Ben-Gurion, primary founder of the state of Israel, James Craig and Jinnah, 'each had the capacity to thwart any alternative proposal', and 'violence or the threat of violence was vital to their success'. What were also common to these partitions were questions of British politics.[33] But there were differences too; unlike with India, Britain did not quit Ireland entirely as Northern Ireland remained a part of the UK and, unlike some other states, the Irish state did not pursue its aim of unity violently. Unionists in Northern Ireland also clung to a siege mentality that could be compared to that of West Bank Zionist settlers.[34]

Neither was the Irish border just about politics or religion; also relevant were 'immemorial' trading patterns and a definition of territory that was social and 'could not be readily flattened out'. Cuilcagh, for example, the mountain where the border reached its highest point, was beyond the reach of customs restrictions and here the sheep of Cavan and Fermanagh could mingle freely.[35] Lillian Spender, on a tour of the border in 1923, exclaimed that 'the beautiful blue mountains of Donegal stood up in the west, cut off from us ... it gave one a strange feeling to see a country so unnaturally and so ungeographically divided, like seeing a living creature cut in two'.[36] In a 1980 poem Paul Muldoon asked

You remember that village where the border ran
Down the middle of the street,
With the butcher and the baker in different states?[37]

Such reflections are a reminder that partition was also a failure of unionism, a nuance subsequently elided by the championing of a unionist version of history that was determined not to complicate the complicated past.[38]

Whatever about these wider contexts and currents, it was the interpretation by the chair of the Boundary Commission, Richard Feetham, a judge of the Supreme Court of the Union of South Africa, that mattered most. The Northern Irish representative on the Commission was Ulster Unionist Joseph Fisher (who wanted to 'get Donegal'), while Eoin MacNeill, the Irish Free State's minister for education, represented the Irish government. MacNeill was a former head of the Irish volunteers who 'appears to have taken literally the decision made by the three that their proceedings be confidential', while Fisher had no such qualms.[39] Crucially, Feetham did not see his task as one of wholesale redrawing of the border: 'Northern Ireland must, when the boundaries have been determined, still be recognisable as the same provincial entity.' He also rejected the idea of plebiscites, and his interpretation amounted to a determination that 'no substantial town could ever be transferred, whatever its population.'[40]

As the Commission prepared its deliberations, the extent to which Ulster could be reunited with the South threw up different perspectives; hardly surprisingly, the poet W. B. Yeats in October 1924 stressed the importance of culture:

I have no hope of seeing a united Ireland in my time, or of seeing Ulster won in my time; but I believe it will be won in the end, and not because we fight it, but because we govern this country well. We can do that, if I may be permitted as an artist and writer to say so, by creating a system of culture which will represent the whole of this country and which will draw the imagination of the young towards it.[41]

But culture, or indeed social and economic considerations, seemed of no concern to the boundary commissioners. What mattered were Feetham's political prejudices, the fact that he was appointed by the British government and the vague wording of the relevant clause in the treaty. Chronicler of the Boundary Commission story Paul Murray makes the point that it is obvious the ambiguities of the clause were very deliberate; if they had not been, they would not have made it to the final text.[42] The Irish side had shown a lack of judgement in leaving such hostages to fortune in 1921. Their view that the counties of Tyrone and Fermanagh as well as large transfers of South Armagh and Newry and Derry City were the prizes on offer was delusional. As early as 16 December 1921 Lloyd George had insisted in the House of Commons that the phrase 'economic and geographic conditions' would not allow for large-scale transfer. The Irish delegation's legal adviser during the treaty negotiations, John O'Byrne, had viewed the text as ambiguous but nonetheless as attorney general in 1925 he still argued that the commissioners were empowered to transfer large swathes of territory.[43]

When the Commission's report was leaked in 1925 it not only revealed that the big prizes north of the border were not on offer but also recommended that a part of east Donegal be transferred to Northern Ireland. The proposal was to shorten the border by 50 miles, transfer 286 square miles to the South and 77 square miles to the North, which would have moved 31,219 people to the Irish Free State and 7,594 in the opposite direction: 'the award of a relatively large portion of South Armagh to the Free State was counterbalanced by the transfer of a rich portion of East Donegal to the North'.[44]

As head of government, W. T. Cosgrave rushed to London to get the report suppressed; the border remained as it was, and as it has done to this day. James Craig was greatly strengthened and he accused the Irish Free State, hardly inaccurately, of having lived in a 'fool's paradise' in believing the Commission would hold out the prospect of Irish unity. Northern nationalists regarded it as a travesty; Cahir Healy, twice elected to the Westminster Parliament in the early 1920s as Sinn Féin MP for Fermanagh and Tyrone, complained that northern nationalists had been 'sold into political servitude for all time'.[45] A measure of the weakness and isolation of Cosgrave was that he could only cry foul because Lloyd George had 'given the impression' of changes to the border favourable to Irish nationalists.

James Craig, in his tour of border areas to reassure his supporters in advance of the Commission's report, had insisted 'what we have, we hold', and following the crisis summit of the three prime ministers in London returned to Belfast in December 'happy and contented'.[46] It was calamitous for Cosgrave but also Eoin MacNeill, who had said, revealingly, he took the job because 'no one else could be found to act instead of me'. He also regarded it as an 'outrage on Ireland' to be asked 'to draw a line across this country dividing it on a basis of religious differences'. But he offered no satisfactory detail on how he handled his role or assessment of whether he could have been more assertive with the Commission and have communicated more effectively with his colleagues about its operation. He seemed to have believed he was involved in a legal rather than political process and did not enlighten his colleagues. It marked the end of his political career.[47]

In the aftermath of this episode there was little looking over the border by the governments on either side. James Craig – who in 1922 had encouraged his brethren to 'remember that the rights of the minority must be sacred to the majority, and that it will only be by broad views, tolerant ideas and a real desire for liberty of conscience that we here can make an ideal of the Parliament and the executive' of Northern Ireland – by 1934 told the Belfast Parliament he was an Orangeman first and a politician and MP afterwards: 'all I boast is that we are a Protestant Parliament and a Protestant State'.[48] Unionist attitudes to that minority (Northern Ireland Catholics comprised 33.5 per cent of the population of the state in 1926) and to the South clearly hardened, and these attitudes were born not of confidence but of insecurity. As a political philosophy unionism did not mature, adapt or evolve beyond a defensive reaction to Irish nationalism and the belief that they were threatened by enemies both within (the Catholic minority) and without (the southern state).[49] Unionists also chose to call elections at times of perceived threat, enabling them to campaign precisely on the border question and stoke reliable embers.

But that southern state was hardly blameless, given its hostility to unionism, its excessive Catholicism (the census of 1926 revealed a southern Irish population that was 92.6 per cent Catholic, which rose to a peak of 94.9 per cent in 1961) and its rhetorically provocative and coarse aspiration to get rid of the border. Dennis Kennedy has highlighted evidence of feelings of discrimination experienced by particular Protestant communities in the Irish Free State, including in Donegal, and argues that violence against the minority in one part of Ireland was often met with reciprocal violence in Northern Ireland, and Craig's insistence that he was an Orangeman first reflected de Valera's earlier claim in 1931 that he was 'a Catholic first'.[50]

Such statements are also a reminder of why, for some nationalists, partition was not seen in negative terms; it could offer an opportunity to generate a 'pure' Irish identity uncontaminated by the 'Black North'. For nationalist journalist D. P. Moran, for example, famed author of *The Philosophy of Irish Ireland* (1905), the treaty offered the opportunity to engage in 'Irishising Ireland' and assert the primacy of its cultural core through use of the Irish language, and this cultural project could transcend questions of sovereignty and partition.[51] He hoped a successful Irish state, culturally and economically confident, could absorb Ulster Protestants on its own terms. But his overriding point was that southern Irish Catholics were now free and 'Gaelicisation' had to take precedence over preoccupation with the border.

That mindset, along with the insistence that Ireland was a single entity, inevitably engendered and encouraged a profound ignorance about Northern Ireland and was 'founded upon evasion, equivocation and ambivalence' which enabled the Irish Free State to simultaneously deny and acknowledge the legitimacy of the northern state.[52] Southerners had no intention of modifying their ideology to fit the new political dispensation and none of the political parties wanted to be blamed for having created or accepted the border. This was perhaps as much psychological as it was political and it involved an eschewing of southern responsibility and no recognition of the legitimacy of unionism. This left the Brits to bash as a safe and acceptable target while the political parties attached the aspiration of unity to their titles; from 1926, Fianna Fáil: The Republican Party and, as successor to Cumann na nGaedheal from 1934, Fine Gael: The United Ireland Party.

Banging the anti-partition drum in the direction of Britain was also a way to avoid any Irish responsibility and the rhetoric decrying partition could be indulged in without any compromise of a nationalist ideology built around the idea of the stolen 'fourth green field' or any talk of the need to persuade unionists about the merits of unity, an approach which inevitably exacerbated the unionist fears and suspicions.[53] There were those, however, who took an independent line, including Ernest Blythe, an Ulster Protestant Sinn Féin TD during the revolutionary era and minister for finance in the 1920s. Reared in Magheragall near Lisburn in County Antrim, a strongly unionist area, he believed in a united Ireland but his background, he suggested, prevented him 'ever falling victim to some of the illusions about partition by which many people in political circles in the South are still fantastically misled and which even continue to influence the minds of many good nationalists in the North'. Any notion of coercion, he believed, was counterproductive, and persuasion was imperative; in 1928 he told the Dáil it needed to prioritise consent.[54]

But there was no such nuance from other establishment quarters. George O'Brien, for example, who was professor of economics in University College Dublin from 1926 and regarded as the pre-eminent economist of his era, wrote a book in 1936 called *The Four Green Fields*, which one of his successors, Patrick Lynch, was later to describe as 'a therapeutic diversion during another breakdown'.[55] He argued that the partition question, largely because of the irredentism of the unionist ascendancy, was insoluble, but that such intractability could be endured alongside friendly relations with Great Britain and the pursuit of economic prosperity in the Irish Free State. He also referred to the 'northern disease' and its containment: 'It would be most regrettable if the sectarian dividing lines between the parties in the North were to spread to the South, and it is hard to see how the infection could be prevented from spreading if the border barrier were destroyed. At the present, sectarianism is safely confined in its Ulster quarantine.'[56]

It would be difficult to find a more self-satisfied example of the partitionist mindset in the South. The irony is that this assertion also came from someone who regarded partition as a national amputation. All this amounted to what Michael Laffan characterised as a 'schizoid' model of identity; southern nationalists 'were less cold and rational than schizoid' and encouraged 'hypoc-risy ... demands were made and poses were struck because of their impact on the South and not on the north'. Ultimately there was also the reality that, in the Irish Free State, 'Partition benefited many people, including some who deplored it' by helping to keep alive a useful anti-Britishness and using anti-partition rhetoric as a convenient rallying cry come elections.[57]

After he broke away from Sinn Féin, Éamon de Valera's Fianna Fáil came to dominate the politics of southern Ireland and sought to secure 'the political independence of a united Ire-land as a republic'. The constitution of 1937, a key initiative of de Valera, contained in Article 2 under the section 'The Nation' the assertion, 'The national territory consists of the whole island of Ireland, its islands and the territorial seas.' Fianna Fáil was able to thrive without making any progress whatsoever on delivering on these aims but the rhetoric remained as a red flag to a Union-ist bull while providing rhetorical reassurance for Fianna Fáil that it was a 'republican' party. Propaganda was the preferred option, with the formation of a Fianna Fáil committee to influence Brit-ish opinion; if the citizens there, de Valera surmised, knew the facts of partition 'it would be inconceivable it would be allowed to remain.'[58]

De Valera, in power 1932–48, 1951–4 and 1957–9, was con-sistent and shallowly stubborn in publicly maintaining the line for decades that Britain had to undo a partition it had imposed, which, to his critics, amounted in practice to a 'do nothing' policy by the dominant Irish political figure of his generation. In 1935, however, he suggested a proposal to end partition centred on an Irish republic with 'local autonomy' for the North East and 'reserved powers going to a central Irish parliament', and guar-antees for the minorities in both parts of the island. This united republic could be 'associated with' the Commonwealth 'on lines of practical co-operation, the fact of co-operation being a sufficient symbol of association' with defence and trade treaties between Ireland and Britain for mutual protection.[59] It came to nothing. In the Senate in 1939, de Valera denied he was a pacifist, and said that he would be justified in using force if he could do so effectively, to 'rescue the people of Tyrone and Fermanagh, South Down, South Armagh and Derry City from the coercion they are suffering'. But he left unanswered the question he asked himself in that speech: 'Would I go further than that?'[60]

De Valera's Anglo-Irish policies in the 1930s and his successful quest to undo the Anglo-Irish Treaty and create a republic in all but name (not formally designated as such because unity had yet to be achieved) created an 'economic war' with Britain when punitive duties were placed on goods in both directions, a development that also made cross-border smuggling more attractive. Between 1932 and 1936 exports from Northern Ireland to the Irish Free State declined by two-thirds and the Control of Manufactures Acts introduced by the Irish government in 1932 and 1934 included regulations preventing firms from Northern Ireland setting up factories in the South.[61]

The re-emergence of tariffs made border smuggling lucrative, and it has been maintained that the 'general web of smuggling' was indulged in to a greater or lesser degree by the majority of the population in the border counties for the simple reason of the border line's 'invisibility'. One despairing Irish Free State customs officer in 1930 asserted 'the people do not seem able to grasp it'; it was, he averred, a 'farce'.[62] But the cattle smugglers certainly grasped it in the 1930s; cattle were the most important export from the Irish Free State, accounting for 35 per cent of the total in 1931. From 1923 to 1932 livestock were non-dutiable, but as a result of the economic war, Britain imposed a 40 per cent duty on livestock and a great increase in smuggling inevitably followed. It was also notable that it was a cross-sectarian practice including those who, in the words of one senior Orange Order man, were members of the Order but 'only worshipped the idol money'. Court appearances for those caught smuggling multiplied: one defendant in July 1933 'denied being concerned in any smuggling and said he generally stopped out til one or two in the morning, reading a novel', which must have been be one of the lamest defences offered and did not prevent him being slapped with a hefty £950 fine.[63]

Cattle were also smuggled by boats on Lough Foyle, lying between counties Derry and Donegal, or by lorry or on foot; another ploy of criminals 'was to pose as policemen or customs officers, to accost the drovers and after the latter had fled, to seize the animals and make off in to the darkness'. The onus of proof lay with the authorities; cattle could not be confiscated or drovers charged unless they were caught red-handed going across the border, which led to 'weary nights of watching, lying in ditch bottoms, sometimes in water or bog land'. A 1934 act shifted the onus of proof to suspects within a twenty-mile border radius; a border patrol of sixty-five men in 1932 was increased to 131 in 1935 and thereafter the Royal Ulster Constabulary, Northern Ireland's police force, was also made available for border duty. There was also smuggling from North to South after 1932, when the Irish Free State imposed duties that raised the price levels of a wide range of consumer goods above that in Northern Ireland, including coats, underwear, shoes, frocks, bread, jam and chocolate. As economic historian D. S. Johnson puts it: 'thanks to the smuggler the partition of Ireland was never quite the economic divide that the official statistics suggest'.[64]

Despite de Valera's foreign policy successes, or perhaps because of them, in particular the return in 1938 of coastal ports that had been retained by Britain for defence under the terms of the Anglo-Irish Treaty, he banged the anti-partition drum whenever possible. He always kept a map of the partitioned island close at hand to impress his views on visitors, but one of the most senior Irish diplomats with long experience of de Valera's attempts to interest London in the issue concluded that de Valera's error was that he believed that partition 'could be solved by logical argument'.[65] John Bowman's *De Valera and the Ulster Question* (1982) depicts him as a pragmatist under considerable pressure from ideological republicans within and outside of his government. But the research of Deirdre McMahon has also uncovered the degree to which some of his fellow ministers thought he needed to be more pragmatic. One of his ministers, Seán MacEntee, a Belfast Catholic, frequently got fed up with de Valera's posturing and intransigence and his frustration is a reminder that there were those within nationalism who felt much of the southern blather was born of a wilful ignorance of the reality of partition.

MacEntee maintained, in a plaintive letter to de Valera in 1938, that the

> partition problem cannot be solved except with the consent of the majority of the Northern non-Catholic population. It certainly cannot be solved by their coercion ... we are relying on Britain's big stick and it will fail ... I have always been prepared in the last resort to defer to your judgement. But I cannot concede that full deference now, because in regard to Partition we have never had a considered policy. It has always been an affair of hasty improvisations, a matter of fits and starts ... we are prepared to subject our farmers and our people as a whole to further and intensified hardship in order to compel Great Britain to force the Northern Non-Catholics to associate with us, when with our connivance every bigot and killjoy, ecclesiastical and lay is doing his damnedest here to keep them out. Where is

the reason in asking us to pursue two policies so utterly at variance with each other? ... some of us are subordinating reason to prejudice ...[66]

British politicians, however, were hardly blameless and too often spoke out of both sides of their mouths. An enduring frustration on the Irish side was that senior British political figures would not match their private sentiment with public rhetoric. John Dulanty, who served as Irish high commissioner in London for twenty years from 1930, wrote to Joseph Walshe, the secretary of the Irish department of external affairs, in May 1934 to inform him that J. H. Thomas, the British dominions secretary, had stated that the British position was that if Northern Ireland chose freely to join the South 'there would of course be no objection but rather satisfaction from the British side'. Two years later Dulanty visited the office of Sir Warren Fisher, permanent secretary to the British Treasury; there was not, suggested Fisher, 'any considerable section of the English people [who] would insist upon the present artificial and absurd boundary of the six counties being made forever permanent. In his view it was a stupid and ludicrous arrangement and if he could end it tomorrow he would do so.'[67]

The same year Joseph Walshe dined with Sir Harry Batterbee, assistant permanent undersecretary of state for dominion affairs, at Walshe's home. Walshe stressed that there was no question of the South attempting to coerce the North 'except in the imagination of some Tory propagandists'. Batterbee had asked the British prime minister Stanley Baldwin to make a statement asserting that Britain would place no obstacle in the way of the establishment of a united Ireland, but Baldwin demurred, as he was worried it would appear too one-sided. Walshe also decried the Northern Ireland government's hostility towards Catholics, 'which had no equal in any civilised society', and insisted that the southern government 'did not tolerate any manifestations of sectarianism in the 26 counties' (which might have been news to some in the confessional South). Walshe also pointed out, 'the majority of our people believed that Great Britain was the real factor in keeping Ireland divided' and 'a great many of our people believed that England regarded the six counties as a sort of bridgehead to be utilised for the reconquest of the rest of Ireland'.[68]

With the outbreak of the Second World War and the declaration of southern Irish neutrality, de Valera was back sparring with his old adversary, Winston Churchill, who had been one of the negotiators of the treaty. From early in his career, Churchill had wrestled with the Irish question in both public and private. As his political thinking evolved, he spoke in favour of Irish self-government and Irish unity, but insisted such unity 'depended on the wooing of Ulster, not its rape'. But there is also an abundance of correspondence and speeches that suggest, in Paul Bew's words, 'the Irish were beyond his comprehension'. He read up on Irish history to a greater extent than most of his contemporaries, but he also saw the Irish as a people who needed to be 'managed' and dealt with 'according to the consciences and conviction of the English people'.[69]

Irish neutrality infuriated Churchill, and by 1939, now back centre stage as First Lord of the Admiralty, he had advised the cabinet 'to take stock of the weapons of coercion' and take back Berehaven in Cork, one of the treaty ports. As British wartime prime minister he was prepared to offer a British declaration accepting the principle of a united Ireland but remained 'consistently irritable' about the subject: 'We must save the people from themselves,' he wrote to Clement Attlee; but 'as always' he 'underestimated the strength of anti-British sentiment in Ireland'.[70] The weakness of Churchill's plan to unite Ireland – a declaration accepting the principle of a united Ireland, a joint body of representatives of the two parts of Ireland to look at the constitutional implications, a joint defence council, and the twenty-six counties joining the war effort – was apparent in this assertion: 'If the plan as a whole is acceptable to the government of Ireland, the United Kingdom government will at once seek to obtain the assent thereto of the government of Northern Ireland, in so far as the plan affects Northern Ireland.'[71]

De Valera did not bite, probably because he was aware that Northern Ireland would react with great hostility, the danger of splitting his own party and the uncertainty about whether Britain would be victorious. His preference was for 'defending the integrity of the existing twenty-six-county state and the unity of Fianna Fáil over what might have been a historic opportunity to undermine partition'. That preference was also reflected in a determination to rout the IRA, still dedicated to fighting for a united Ireland, with a membership of between 10,000 and 12,000 and which had been declared an unlawful organisation by a Fianna Fáil government in June 1936. Seven IRA men were executed by army firing squad during the war; three others were allowed to die on hunger strike, while more than 500 were interned without trial and another 600 were committed under the Offences Against the State Act, which became law in June 1939. The essential issue for de Valera was the legitimacy of the southern state, particularly because, in his own words, 'there were no longer any obstacles in the way of any section to utilising constitutional means'.[72]

Flushed with drink and euphoria after the Pearl Harbor attack in 1941, Churchill dispatched a telegram to de Valera: 'Now or Never. A Nation Once Again'. It was judiciously ignored and unionists got on with their business of embracing the Allied cause. Paul Bew has highlighted the text of another telegram, to Anthony Eden in September 1943, in which Churchill suggested:

There will be no difficulty in resisting the partition argument so long as Southern Ireland stands out of the War. If, on the other hand she comes into the War, great changes of feeling might occur both in the North of Ireland and in the British mind. As one who has always been in favour of United Ireland into which the North has willingly entered I would view such an evolution without alarm.[73]

But as George Bernard Shaw, the renowned Irish playwright resident in England, saw it during the Second World War, because Britain swallowed de Valera's insistence it would not get the treaty ports, and settled for using Northern Ireland as a base for Allied operations, de Valera 'was saved by the partition which he abhorred' and that 'powerless little cabbage garden called Erin, wins'.[74] It seemed, in Shaw's words, a 'crack-brained line to take' but de Valera 'got away with it'.[75]

The war underlined the starkly different political priorities and affiliations of the two Irish states and reinforced the border (while de Valera sent southern fire brigades to Belfast when it was being blitzed by the Germans in April and May 1941, this humanitarian gesture was undermined in unionist eyes by his simultaneous assertion 'we are one and the same people'). Unlike its neutral southern counterpart, the Northern Ireland government was fully committed to the war effort, and suffered in ways the South was mostly spared, but that did not mean that Northern Ireland's relations with London were always smooth. At the start of the war, James Craig's wife recorded in her diary that the British prime minister, Neville Chamberlain, had forced Craig to back down in relation to his demand that conscription be extended to Northern Ireland: 'If you really want to help us, don't press for conscription. It will only be an embarrassment.'[76] Conscription was not imposed, a reminder of the degree to which Northern Ireland was seen as a special case within the UK. In 1945, James Craig's successor as prime minister, Basil Brooke, insisted that national service should be extended to Northern Ireland in order to, among other things, confirm the state's constitutional status within the Union, but when the National Service Bill was introduced at Westminster in 1946, Northern Ireland was excluded.

Smugglers had a busy war criss-crossing the border, given rationing. Eggs and sugar were brought north, with tea and petrol making their way south. Rationing continued well after the war and into the 1950s, 'which sustained the market for petty smugglers with an entrepreneurial flair'. One elderly Irish woman who regularly visited relatives across the border in Derry 'travelled by train, because you had far more train connections in those days, and for her comfort had a hot water bottle'. However, the bottle she clutched was reputedly filled with whiskey, which was 'readily available in the South but heavily rationed in the North ... She would take that to a relative on the Northern Ireland side of the border. For the return journey, she would fill the bottle with tea leaves, which were very scarce in the South of Ireland.'[77]

Another aspect of the border question during the Second World War was the social attractiveness of the South, given the more exacting restrictions in wartime North; consider, for example, the advertisement that appeared in the *Belfast Telegraph* in December 1939 on the back of the Irish Tourist Association's Christmas campaign, designed to lure visitors over the border: 'Dublin has no BLACK-OUT! Dublin is the gayest city in Ireland this Christmas – no black-out, a carefree atmosphere, and all entertainments in full swing ... why not make this a Christmas of fun and merriment, instead of black-out boredom and irksome restrictions?'[78]

By the end of the 1940s de Valera had emphatically rejected force as a means to end partition and seemed to acknowledge that the problem was one between the North and South of Ireland, and not Britain: 'If there were agreement between the peoples of the two parts of Ireland, British consent to do the things that they would have to do could be secured.'[79] Violence, he knew, even if it achieved a united Ireland, could achieve only a temporary, unstable outcome.[80]

But by then he was out of power, following Fianna Fáil's defeat in the 1948 general election after sixteen years in office. The new coalition government led by Taoiseach John A. Costello of Fine Gael included a new quasi-republican party, Clann na Poblachta, led by former IRA chief-of-staff Seán MacBride (who became minister for external affairs), Labour, farmers and independents. De Valera embarked on an indulgent international anti-partition tour that achieved nothing, during which he insisted unionists would have to decide whether they were British or Irish. Hugh Delargy, chairman of the Anti-Partition of Ireland League in Britain, suggested the tour meetings there 'were all flops ... they were tribal rallies; tribesmen met to greet the old chieftain'.[81] The tour could not have come at a worse time in terms of interesting a wider world recovering from the Second World War.

A propaganda machine, under the auspices of the Mansion House Committee, was also set up by the coalition government in 1949, a reminder that Fianna Fáil did not have a monopoly on anti-partition evangelism and there was much jostling for position to prove anti-partition credentials. Costello averred that he considered himself prime minister of all Ireland, 'no matter what the Irish in the North say', and called a meeting of leaders of the southern parties and northern nationalists to provide support for anti-partition candidates in the looming Northern Ireland elections (with a countrywide collection outside churches) at which the Mansion House Committee was established. It was, in reality, a boon to unionists; a northern nationalist was quoted as saying, 'Those fellows in Dublin are playing party politics, and that is not going to help us.'[82] He was correct. Nationalist seats actually fell from ten to nine, the Labour movement was sidelined and the Ulster Unionists increased their representation from thirty-three to thirty-seven seats in the fifty-two-seat Northern Ireland Parliament.

Nationalists in Derry had no grounds for optimism; Paddy Maxwell, Nationalist MP for Foyle, suggested one could not talk of a Nationalist Party in the North 'in the sense in which parties are understood in other places'. Since partition it had been impossible to maintain any kind of unified political organisation: for too long they had 'allowed themselves to be divided, thus preventing their case against partition being properly presented at home and abroad'.[83] Eddie McAteer, elected MP for mid-Derry in 1945, was instrumental in the foundation of the Irish Anti-Partition League, which sought to build a coalition of former republicans, contemporary nationalists and their southern counterparts. McAteer wrote the foreword to the League's publication *Ireland's Fascist City* in 1946 in relation to the gerrymandering of the corporation of Derry: 'every single day the Irish nationalist majority in this Irish city are robbed of their elementary democratic rights'.[84]

The logic was that, unless they united, northern nationalists could do little to end partition, but the argument also had to be taken to Britain, a Britain that was not remotely interested. McAteer had hoped that a Labour government under Clement Attlee might be sympathetic, but that was wishful thinking.

However, some nationalists were conflicted. That same decade writer Benedict Kiely, who grew up in Omagh, announced at the beginning of *Counties of Contention* (1945): 'The attempt to appreciate Unionist sentiment will possibly offend a few Nationalist Irishmen; while the inevitable result of the writer's nationalist breeding and background will eventually drive away all but the most impartial and persevering Unionist readers.'[85]

Kiely characterised unionism as a defence of ascendancy that was sustained by appeals to Protestant 'persecution mania' and 'that reconciliation and an end to partition are necessary to save the whole island from mediocrity'.[86] A strong believer in the unifying power of culture, Kiely was no rabid, unthinking republican: 'If I were given the choice tomorrow between the continuance of partition and a one government Ireland ruling the Protestants of Ulster against their will I would choose a partitioned Ireland.'[87] But, as an *Irish Times* reviewer concluded, 'every book and every speech about partition, unfortunately, tends to harden the will of the Protestants of Ulster against partition'.[88]

Partition was also a divisive issue for the Labour Party in Northern Ireland (NILP), and that party could hardly share the naïve insistence of George Bernard Shaw that Ulster Protestant capitalism would never yield to southern republican agitation, but would undo partition when it was outvoted by organised labour 'and could fortify itself against socialism' only by an alliance with the agricultural capitalists of the South.[89]

Harry Midgley, chairman of the party and styled as a workers' champion, made a 'declaration of policy' in November 1942, which committed the NILP to supporting Northern Ireland's constitutional position within the UK. It inevitably created a rift as there were also anti-partitionists and those neutral on the matter in the party, and Midgely resigned from the party the following month, launching the Commonwealth Labour Party, of which he was to be the sole parliamentary representative. Midgely had a toxic relationship with another leading Ulster Labour figure, Jack Beattie, who had strong nationalist sympathies; they even exchanged blows in the Stormont Parliament in October 1945. Therein lay the dilemma for Labour and the border; it could not transcend partition in the interests of island-wide socialism as it got pulled into the unionist/nationalist trenches.

Despite the 'greening' of the first coalition government of 1948–51, the same frustrations and flights of fancy experienced by its predecessor governments were often apparent in relation to its stance on the border. Seán MacBride sought to champion a radical new social republicanism and Ireland's departure from the Commonwealth. This happened in 1949 after John A. Costello announced the government's intention to repeal the External Relations Act, 1936, under which the king signed the credentials of Irish ambassadors, the last remaining formal link with the Commonwealth, thus making southern Ireland a republic. The British government had not been informed and was distinctly unimpressed as Costello wrapped the green flag around himself and made it clear this was not done at the behest of MacBride. Costello suggested the declaration of the Irish Republic would help take the gun out of Irish politics and end a provocation for republicans, after which Northern Ireland prime minister Basil Brooke (1943–63) announced 'we have now on our southern border a foreign nation'.[90]

But Costello may also have had other, more parochial priorities, principally to provide a refutation to the idea that Fine Gael was a 'pro-British party'. Either way, it resulted in a British retaliation in the form of the Ireland Act of 1949, which declared, 'In no event will Northern Ireland or any part thereof cease to be part ... of the United Kingdom without the consent of the Parliament of Northern Ireland.' This act can be attributed to resentment on the part of Britain about lack of consultation about the declaration of the Irish Republic as well as Attlee's acceptance that Brooke's distrust of southern nationalist intentions was justified.

The advice from a British government working party was that Northern Ireland's continued inclusion within the UK was vital for British strategic interests. Its report affirmed, 'It will never be to Great Britain's advantage that Northern Ireland should form part of a territory outside His Majesty's jurisdiction. Indeed it seems unlikely that Great Britain would ever be able to agree to this even if the people of Northern Ireland desired it.'[91] Historian Jonathan Bardon has described the Ireland Act as 'shoring up the Unionist position ... and the whole episode left them in a position more impregnable than ever before in the twentieth century'.[92] Con Cremin, Irish Ambassador to Britain from 1956 to 1958, recalled that it had always been felt in Ireland that the Labour Party was friendly to Ireland, so there had been much upset at the 'quite gratuitous' inclusion of the offending clause in the Ireland Bill: 'this in effect means the situation is frozen indefinitely'.[93]

It was easy for certain senior British figures to say privately they would like to see Ireland united but that it was a problem for Ireland to solve. MacBride wrote to the lord chancellor, Lord Jowitt, in October 1948 to say he was 'terribly glad and happy' that Jowitt was in favour of ending partition, but

> I cannot altogether agree that it is a matter that concerns only the North and South of Ireland ... it is difficult to convince the people on this side that Britain is not involved. They have no way of reading into the minds of your statesmen ... I do accept that members of the present British government desire in an academic fashion to see it solved, but they have done nothing.[94]

MacBride also complained in March 1949, in a letter to Frank Pakenham, Minister for Civil Aviation and strongly sympathetic to the Irish nationalist case against partition, that in dealing with the British government he was never 'quite certain of the grounds upon which they refuse to face up to the partition question'. He felt it could not be on its merits, so it must have been 'on grounds of expediency'. Once the Irish government could sit around a

table with the 'six-county Tories ... I do not think that the finding of a solution will be so very difficult ... our friends in the six
counties do a good deal of blustering but I think that they realise
that the ending of partition is inevitable'.[95] That, it turned out, was
a severe underestimation of Ulster unionism. He did, however,
identify the crux of the problem; the British government 'always
give me the impression of being too busy to be bothered about
this question' and demonstrated a 'complete lack of understanding and interest'.[96]

Two years later in London, Irish ambassador Fred Boland
was excited about a debate on partition in the House of Commons, but it turned out to be no such thing and it achieved 'little
or nothing from our point of view'. The Labour Party instead
focused on 'six-county Toryism', not partition: 'the damaging
implication was that if there were a better government at Stormont everything would be lovely in the garden'. Neither did it suit
Ireland to have a focus on sectarianism because it allowed Britain to present itself as able to, in Boland's words, 'hold the scales
evenly between two irreconcilably antagonistic religious sects'.[97]
This suited both of the main British parties and there seemed little divergence between them when it came to the Irish border; the
deputy prime minister, Herbert Morrison, had summed this up in
1949 by asserting that Ireland 'ought not to be a deciding factor in
British politics' and that partition was a matter for both parts of
Ireland.[98]

Crucially, the constitutional changes that occurred in the late
1940s in relation to the Anglo-Irish question were not the result
of bilateral negotiations; such distancing brought about 'the failure of mutual comprehension' and the 'facility to generate mutual
mistrust'.[99] Nor were Northern Ireland politicians spared English
resentment at the intrusion of the Irish question. In the House
of Commons in July 1954 Aneurin Bevan of the Labour Party

lacerated Northern Ireland's MPs for their 'meagre contribution to debate', their 'deplorable level of parliamentary representation' and their 'old fashioned arguments', contending that, due to the 'extent to which they are obviously under the influence of vested interests in Northern Ireland ... we ourselves ought no longer to be oppressed by their presence and have our legislative process interfered with by their votes'.[100]

3

Old Fantasies, New Perspectives and a Gentle Thaw

Irish governments' approaches to the border question were consistent in the 1950s and remained remarkably weak regardless of who was in government. Frank Aiken, born in County Armagh in 1898, was minister for external affairs from 1951 to 1954, and from 1957 to 1969, a tenure that has not been surpassed in length, so it is especially notable that he had such limited horizons and exceptional callowness, bordering on the childlike, when it came to the border question. In July 1951 he authored a secret memorandum in which he referred to meeting a number of British politicians and urging them to make a declaration 'that it was a British interest that Ireland should be united ... I told them I did not care whether they wanted to see a united Ireland or not, or whether in fact they were personally against unity so long as they recognised and said publicly that it was a British interest that it should be united'.

What was astonishing, however, was the blind immaturity of a senior politician who was a veteran of the Irish war of independence and civil war: he suggested if British politicians acceded to his request 'the people in Belfast would know that the days of partition were numbered and from that time forth relations between ourselves and Britain would improve and between ourselves and the six counties'.[1] It was as if the history of the previous five decades had never happened; the idea that Ulster unionists would embrace the Republic in the context of what would certainly be seen as a gross British portrayal was farcical.

Britain persisted with the attitude that the border issue was a problem that needed to be solved by the two parts of Ireland (only to insist the following decade that it was an internal British matter). In 1952 Fred Boland, Irish ambassador in London, was told by Winston Churchill that the Republic must 'woo the North', a phrase also used by Anthony Eden. The same year, Aiken met with the leader of the House of Lords: 'I said that partition was going to come to an end, that it was too artificial to last'; Lord Salisbury gave no ground, but Aiken described the interview as candid and 'free flowing and friendly', which was just as well, given that Aiken had also asserted that 'the British were a queer people'.[2]

The level of Aiken's fantasy was also underlined by a memorandum from Conor Cruise O'Brien, a counsellor in the Department of External Affairs. O'Brien was convinced that, 'unless we can bring division among our adversaries and above all dislocate the "Protestant solidarity" on which the Stormont regime has been so firmly based ... no amount of pressure from outside can bring about what we desire'. Ireland needed to add to the 'existing strains' in the Orange Order and the Unionist Party, though he accepted that, while systematic disenfranchisement of and discrimination against nationalists was abhorrent, 'expressions like "Fascist Tyranny" and "Iron Curtain conditions"' were not 'particularly helpful'.[3]

It is striking how much of the energy of the Department of External Affairs was sapped by the anti-partition rhetorical crusade at a time when there were changes afoot internationally in relation to European integration and the challenging of nationalist shibboleths. Aiken was obsessional, it seemed, about the moral superiority of Ireland's anti-partition case, but he was not interested in understanding unionism. Cruise O'Brien promoted the government's case but was much more nuanced than Aiken; he was well aware that haranguing the British government to 'hand over' Northern Ireland was a doomed project: 'therefore the main field on which we must always keep our eye is the Six Counties area itself'.[4]

Nor was there much solace in the USA for those who sought the removal of the border, and America was not minded to forgive and forget Irish neutrality during the war. Joseph D. Brennan, Irish ambassador in Washington, complained in 1948 of the 'extraordinary amount of prejudice which exists against us ... they fear that if partition was abolished they would not have the facilities available to them in our country which they would like and they are sure of such facilities in the Six Counties'.[5] Two years later Brennan waded instead into mushy piety in insisting that Ireland was entitled to have its anti-partition crusade embraced by the wider Western world; Irish fighters for freedom had in the 1920s 'saved the soul of Ireland alive. But the body of our nation had, in the fearful ordeal of force, been smashed by the mailed fist of the tyrant and part of it was still held in its iron grasp. Ireland belongs to the Atlantic community. She is a co-founder of western civilisation.'[6]

John J. Hearne, Irish ambassador in the US from 1950 to 1960, composed a lengthy memorandum in September 1951 lamenting that, unlike with the situation during the war of independence, 'no great national organisation has been called into existence to further the cause ... the issue of Irish national unity has never been blazed across the American continent as the issue of Irish national independence was blazed thirty years ago'. This was a disappointment as the anti-partition campaign had been up and running for two years; as Paul O'Dwyer, the Irish-born New York Democrat, saw it, 'the ignorance of the vast majority of Americans on Ireland and what the partition problem is all about is beyond belief'. Nor did American politicians regard partition as a sufficient reason for Ireland staying outside of NATO.[7]

An American League for an Undivided Ireland had been formed in 1947 but it really only consisted of 'a number of key men in various cities' and it had 'no offices, no secretariat and no register of membership'. Hearne nonetheless indulged in the ardour beloved of that generation that suggested the world torch should shine on Ireland by natural right: 'the higher principles involved in our position are lost sight of or make no appeal ... the partition of Ireland by force by an outside power ought to be the concern of all other peoples'. It was about the 'seamless garment of our nationality'. But there were also uncomfortable realities amidst the soaring dreams: some members of the House of Representatives made it known that 'many young men and young women emigrating from Ireland to the US have shown no enthusiasm for national reunion'.[8] A slightly more sober Taoiseach John A. Costello composed a memo following his visit to the US in March 1956 and argued that membership of the UN (which the Republic joined in 1955) was the way to make progress on partition: 'if we conduct ourselves well and intelligently at the UN and in America generally we may hope gradually to create conditions in which, through the influence of our friends, partition may be brought to an end. Partition cannot be ended without friends and friendship cannot be won by an entirely selfish policy.'[9]

But what was also very revealing was the (continuing) disdain with which northern nationalists felt they were treated by the southern political establishment. In September 1955, when John Belton of the Department of External Affairs made a visit to meet northern nationalists, he was made well aware not only of their divisions but also of their complaints of 'lack of leadership' from Dublin and a general 'recognition that there is no early prospect of ending partition.'[10]

In the early 1950s northern Nationalist MPs requested seats in the Dáil but the Irish government rejected their demand. With characteristic bluntness Eddie McAteer retorted: 'Evidently, the two main parties in the Dáil are determined that no reproachful voice from the North will disturb their Kathleen Mavourneen policy on partition.'[11] The Irish government similarly denied his own request for 'a right of audience' in the southern legislature.[12] McAteer's reference to Kathleen Mavourneen was taken from an 1830s song, which included the lyrics

> Kathleen Mavourneen what slumbering still
> Oh hast thou forgotten how soon we must sever?
> Oh hast thou forgotten the day we must part?
> It may be for years and it may be forever
> Oh why art thou silent thou voice of my heart?[13]

Costello hid behind talk of the disunity of nationalists and constitutional and legal difficulties against them being heard in the republic's Parliament and the possibility that Nationalist representatives might use the Dáil chamber to advocate force, but he also maintained that if Northern Ireland prime minister Basil Brooke 'and some of his colleagues expressed the smallest desire to have a right of audience in the Dáil ... we could immediately take steps to amend the Constitution or to pass any necessary Act in five minutes to let them come down here.'[14] Nor was Fianna Fáil brimming with any welcome or enthusiasm. As independent senator Roger McHugh put it, 'Deputy de Valera's cranky query as to what was the point of people coming in here to discuss Partition reflects the same mentality and tends to produce the impression of vested political interests on this side of the Border who do not want any interference with the status quo.'

But another Independent senator, Owen Sheehy Skeffington, also raised the issue of welfare in a very direct way:

> the social services, the rates of pay, subsidies and so on. The Six County farmer, the Six County unskilled and semi-skilled worker, the Six County teacher, the Six County housewife and the Six County school child all get ... far more effective and generous aid, Catholic and Protestant alike, than we find possible to give to their brothers and sisters down here ... I want to make the point, when we are asking for the removal of the Border, and asking our friends in the North of Ireland to come down here to give us their views, and giving them audience, that we want to be able to know ... what we can offer them, and what sacrifices, if any, we have to ask them to make.[15]

Northern Ireland had got its welfare state, pioneered by the Labour Party in Britain by extending access to health, housing and education, not because Britain was so keen to extend it but because it was regarded as politically dangerous to exclude Northern Ireland from its benefits. The Catholic Church went to great lengths to oppose less sweeping measures in the Republic, especially in health, and there was a furore over attempts to introduce a state-funded scheme of maternal and infant care in 1951. The same Church accepted the welfare state in Northern Ireland with only 'token complaints'.[16] Noel Browne, the controversial young minister for health in 1948 seeking to extend the state's reach in health care in the Republic, faced opposition from Catholic bishops, but when he dined with Cardinal John D'Alton, the Catholic primate of all Ireland, D'Alton 'made no attempt to answer the one crucial and pertinent question that I did put to him about the use of Aneurin Bevan's National Health Service by Catholics in Northern Ireland. His disdainful reply smacked of royalty standing on its dignity: "We are prepared neither to apologise, nor to explain."[17]

What other social differences were relevant to the border divide and what did both parts of Ireland have in common? Intermediate education was provided for all in the late 1940s in Northern Ireland but free secondary education was not introduced in the Republic until 1967. There were housing problems in both states, but it was worse in the South: in 1926, 27.7 per cent of its population were categorised as living in overcrowded conditions compared to 18.1 per cent in Northern Ireland. Marriage between different denominations was frowned upon in both jurisdictions; since 1908 the Catholic decree *Ne Temere* stipulated that mixed religious couples had to formally agree, in writing, that their children would be raised as Catholics, which was greatly resented by the Protestant churches, though in Northern Ireland 'marriage even between different Protestant denominations was frowned upon well into the twentieth century'.[18] While divorce was obtainable in the North but prohibited in the South, similar views prevailed on both sides of the border in relation to understanding of the family as a 'conservative, rural, Christian and patriarchal unit'.[19]

The violence focused on the border by the late 1950s was another political challenge, particularly with the IRA's campaign of 1956–62. By the mid 1940s many had believed the IRA had lost all potency, but it re-emerged with the ill-conceived and ultimately disastrous 'border campaign', having formally decided to avoid hostilities in the twenty-six counties and instead aim at border targets. One of the best-known fatalities of the campaign was Seán South, a young Limerick man who had come to believe in the necessity for another 1916 Rising for Ireland to redeem its soul. On the early evening of 1 January 1957 he was in the fourteen-man contingent that raided the RUC barracks at Brookeborough, County Fermanagh. After South and another even younger IRA man, Fergal O'Hanlon, were killed there followed 'a week of all but national mourning'. On 4 January large crowds lined the route of South's funeral cortège from Monaghan town – where O'Hanlon had been buried earlier in the day – 'down the east coast through Dublin and across the country to Limerick, where 20,000 mourners, including the city's mayor, received the remains at midnight'.[20] The death of O'Hanlon inspired 'The Patriot Game', an iconoclastic song by Dominic Behan:

My name is O'Hanlon, I'm just gone sixteen
My home is in Monaghan there I was weaned
I learned all my life cruel England to blame
And so I'm part of the patriot game
This Ireland of mine has for long been half-free
Six Counties are under John Bull's Monarchy
But still de Valera is greatly to blame
For shirking his part in the patriot game[21]

Such songs, the empathetic reaction to the border campaign deaths and the resentment directed at politicians deemed to be insufficiently militant underlined that, thirty-seven years after the creation of the border, it could still generate an emotive response, but it was just a transient vehemence. A pamphlet recalling the attack on the Brookeborough Barracks sold 10,000 copies in a month shortly afterwards.[22] But the Irish electorate showed little interest in supporting Sinn Féin in the South. By March 1958 there were 131 republicans in the Curragh internment camp in Kildare and in the general election of 1961 in the Republic Sinn Féin lost the four seats it had won in the 1957 election, suggesting that at the outset of a new decade, it had little appealing to say to an audience in the South concerned not about partition, but about social and economic issues.

Sinn Féin's poor showing in that 1961 election was reacted to with an expression of moral superiority by the republican *United Irishman* newspaper; voters who had prioritised economic concerns over the ending of partition were castigated as 'selfish little materialists'.[23] The IRA was thus forced to rethink the Republic because its political identity was misty and incoherent (Irish republicanism was self-described as 'Christian, republican and democratic'[24]) and the IRA was riven with factions over the border campaign. Certainly the campaign stirred the Fianna Fáil grass roots and there was concern about the need for the party to 'speak in the same voice' in condemning the IRA at a time when some in the party were vocal in calling for the release of IRA prisoners. But in truth the campaign was never going to ignite national sentiment in a way that would transform the status quo and the IRA statement announcing its end in February 1962 was very telling: 'Foremost among the factors responsible for the ending of the campaign has been the attitude of the general pubic whose minds have been deliberately distracted from the supreme issue facing Irish people – the unity and freedom of Ireland.'[25] It was a fanciful and arrogant end.

As Taoiseach from 1959 to 1966, Seán Lemass, who replaced de Valera, was quick to tell his colleagues impatiently that irredentist anti-partition rhetoric could not hide the fact that Northern Ireland existed with the consent of the majority of its inhabitants. He even admitted to the British ambassador in 1959 that Irish governments had made many mistakes in relation to Northern Ireland. He discouraged the use of the term 'six counties', though recognising the constitutional status of Northern Ireland was not yet deemed to be feasible. Lemass had been frustrated that de Valera would not row in behind the idea of a new economic approach to Northern Ireland by removal of trade barriers, but as leader Lemass had more leeway and a memorandum approved by him looked at the need for more economic co-operation. Lemass and some others in Fianna Fáil began to deliver speeches that tentatively offered de facto recognition of Northern Ireland, but Lemass continued an ambiguity by occasionally still nodding in a more traditional direction.

Nonetheless, there were undoubtedly some new perspectives on the border from the 1950s that stood in complete contrast to the logic of the IRA's border campaign. Writer Hubert Butler, often vocal about the need for southern Protestants, of which he was one, to be a more vocal minority, began to organise debates between Ulster unionists and southern nationalists in 1954. He wrote about crossing the border the following year, suggesting it was 'more of an obsession than it need be ... we have been hypnotised into believing that there is a real barrier there and, like those neurotic hens which can be kept from straying by drawing a chalk ring round them, we do not venture across'. An essential preliminary to any union, he argued, was 'free and friendly intercourse' but 'too many people would sooner be silent or untruthful than disloyal to their side'.[26]

Ernest Blythe also continued to write extensively on the subject of partition; his book *Briseadh na Teorann* (The Smashing of the Border) (1955) did not make as much of an impact as it might have if it had been in English but it was robustly demythifying. The basis for partition, he suggested, was not British presence in Northern Ireland but unionist demand for it based on religious difference and the resultant politico-sectarian segregation. Southern coercion and threat could only reinforce that divide; what was needed was persuasion of sufficient Protestants to vote for reunion. The 'internal-conflict' paradigm, or the idea of a 'divided society', was a novel interpretation at that stage.[27]

It was, however, soon to gain considerable currency. Young southern writer Michael Sheehy joined the chorus the same year with *Divided We Stand*, disputing the argument that partition was caused by British policy:

> the Irish community has never adopted a sane and realistic view of the problem caused by its division [partition]. It has never been willing to allow the Northern Protestant community independent and separate rights so as to make Irish unity a question of voluntary agreement on the basis of a frank discussion of the problems involved in unity ... The Irish community has, indeed, completely ignored the fact that the division of Ireland is the result of a fundamental internal spiritual opposition. Such an attitude distorts the essential character of the problem of Partition and makes its solution a practical impossibility.[28]

In 1957 Donal Barrington, later a Supreme Court judge, in *Uniting Ireland*, also deplored the impoverishment of nationalist thinking about the border because it simply blamed Britain and insisted it must undo partition. This, he suggested, was convenient sloganeering that overlooked the extent to which the border had been created by the conflicting demands of Irishmen and was a lazy propaganda that was incendiary in the hands of those intent on attacking the border: 'Surely', he wrote 'it is time we faced the fact that our country is divided and is in danger of remaining divided forever?' More stingingly, he suggested 'all the policies which the South has adopted in the past thirty-five years with a view to ending partition have, in fact, tended to strengthen and perpetuate it'.[29] Partition could not be ended, the argument extended, without the consent of the Northern Ireland Parliament.

Garret FitzGerald, future Fine Gael Taoiseach, described this as 'the first major challenge to traditional irredentist anti-partitionism' (which was hardly true, given the work of Blythe and Sheehy) while, later, Fianna Fáil minister and future president of Ireland Erskine Childers suggested it encouraged a thaw in the cold war between North and South.[30] It is likely the efficacious secretary of the Department of Finance appointed the previous year, T. K. Whitaker (born in County Down), was also influenced by it, and he went on to be a key influence on southern policy towards Northern Ireland from the 1960s.

There was, concomitantly, a more prosaic focus on possible agreements with the government of Northern Ireland in relation to, for example, Lough Foyle, the Erne fisheries and the Dublin–Belfast railway, hardly the stuff of 'A Nation Once Again' and not what Joseph D. Brennan would have had in mind as just reward for co-founding Western civilisation. But the Lough Foyle fishing war, which had raged in previous decades and ended only with the establishment of the Foyle Fishery Commission by joint legislation of both Irish parliaments in 1952, had been exceptionally toxic with rival claims to the tidal waters of the Foyle and included numerous 'nocturnal surprises and reprisals'. Cases that came before the courts about this issue demonstrated that 'neither fishermen, customs officers, fishery inspectors nor the legal profession could say with any certitude where the boundary lay'. The resultant commission was the first cross-border body with decision-making powers.[31]

Nor was the border just about politics, religion, violence or economics; it was also about psychology. Irish poet Celia de Fréine has written powerfully of what it meant for her and her family in the 1950s and 1960s. Her parents moved from the North to Dublin shortly after she was born:

I grow up, knowing they're lonely and isolated from their families, and that their accents are different from everyone else's. Dublin is bleak and miserable; though, unlike in the North, its parks open on Sundays and the swings and slides are never padlocked. There are sweets when there is money to buy them, though not the same selection as in the North where Maltesers, Bounty bars, and Spangles can be purchased.[32]

But on visits to Northern Ireland, she discovers that a Protestant child she befriends 'has had to be given special permission by her church to play with me, a Roman Catholic', and this ends when a Protestant friend is found for the Protestant girl ('I never saw her again').[33]

Given the preponderance of such religious divides, how vocal were Church leaders about the border? The intervention in 1957 of John Francis D'Alton, appointed archbishop of Armagh (and thus Catholic primate of all Ireland) in 1946 and a cardinal in 1953 was notable. Unlike his predecessors in the previous hundred years, Dalton was not an Ulster man but born in Mayo. D'Alton regularly condemned partition: 'As a lover of my country I naturally deplore the political partition of this island of ours which God intended to be one and individual.' Where D'Alton was unusual was in suggesting a solution involving each of the six Ulster counties deciding individually whether to remain with the southern or northern state (the so called 'county option'). In turn, whether or not to join the Commonwealth could be decided by an Ireland united in a federation (an independent republic that would associate itself with the Commonwealth on the same basis as India) under which the Stormont government would give to the Dublin government the same allegiance it gave to Westminster, with any intention to join the NATO alliance decided by plebiscite.

Those who saw merit and more in his proposals regarded them as 'too little studied and too soon forgotten'.[34] His Protestant counterpart, Dr James McCann, was effusive in his praise for him after he died in 1963; D'Alton had worked hard, McCann suggested, to create 'good feeling amongst the various members of the community'. McCann made his own contribution by insisting 'denominationalism is outmoded', in contrast to another Northern Ireland church leader from that era, Ian Paisley, who thrived on anti-Catholic tirades and exacerbated splits over theology in the Presbyterian Church in the early 1950s in order to grow his Free Presbyterian flock. The *Irish Times* reminded that the position D'Alton held 'is not, because of our history, an easy one. It calls for diplomacy as well as devotion.'[35] But if it was true that D'Alton was careful, dignified and respected, it was also evident that there was a pointed silence from politicians about his proposals. When he made his comments in March 1957 there was a general election in the Republic and neither leader of government, Costello, or opposition, de Valera, chose to respond despite being asked. Amusingly, the cardinal insisted his comments had been made in a personal capacity 'as an Irishman' and 'he did not wish to become involved in politics', as if such an exclusion were remotely possible when making an intervention about partition as Catholic Archbishop of Armagh.[36]

The main points made by D'Alton were published in *The Observer* newspaper and there was also an economic dimension to them; the idea that a united Ireland could make a contribution to the solution of problems raised by the proposed free-market area of Europe. The *Irish Times* suggested that 'in recent months there has been an awareness in political circles that many important political minds were thinking on new lines about partition, the commonwealth, relations with other European nations and with the United States'.[37]

The Ulster Unionist chief whip at Stormont, Brian Faulkner, a future prime minister, insisted in responding to the 'county option' idea, 'we are not prepared to discuss any constitutional arrangement which will take us out of the United Kingdom', and he noted that 'Irish republican overtures' to Ulster had varied from threatened force, to force, to 'sweetly reasonable'. He also maintained, in a self-serving bastardisation of history, that it was 'Eire's decision to go into isolation in 1921 which created partition'.[38]

Interestingly, when revisiting D'Alton's suggestion in 1965, unionist prime minister Terence O'Neill (1963–9) chose to focus on the economic argument: 'who is going to pay for our welfare state in a United Ireland? We do really value our British welfare state. It is something of real importance to us in the North. It brings benefits to all people here ... I can see no economic advantage whatsoever in joining with Eire.'[39]

O'Neill did, however, welcome Seán Lemass over the border in 1965 and then made the crossing himself. O'Neill liked to present cross-border dialogue with Lemass as possible 'because of the strength of our constitutional position'. The meetings undoubtedly represented a thaw in the Irish cold war but this was also accompanied by an ongoing disdain on Lemass's part for northern nationalists' failure to engage in northern politics; he privately derided them as 'old women' and found them as 'intractable' as their unionist counterparts.[40]

Historian Joe Lee has pointed out that, for Lemass, 'the emergence of the EEC and of the European Free Trade Association enabled him to plead the pressures of international reality as a justification for adapting domestic policy to changed circumstances' and that, with economic expansion in the Republic through its embrace of free trade, the widening 'gap in living standards between north and south' enabled him to present 'economic growth as an essential step on the road to unification'.[41]

Lemass held out a hand to unionists while also arguing that economic success would remove one of the main unionist objections to Irish unification: 'There are people today in the North-east of the country who say that we are here paying an uneconomic price for our freedom. We have got to prove them wrong.' In 1961 he had contrasted the 'dynamism' of the Republic with increased unemployment in the North and resultant begging missions by Northern Ireland's prime minister to London: 'We are proving that there are better ways of dealing with the country's problems than by sending deputations to plead for help from others. The bread of charity is never very filling. I am convinced that the success of our economic programme can be a decisive factor in bringing about the change of outlook which the North requires and the discarding of all the old fallacies and prejudices on which partition has rested.'[42]

For O'Neill, under pressure to reform unionism, who used the description 'bridge-building' and watched a hurling match with nuns in 1964 to display the supposed depth of his new empathy with the Ulster Gaels, the meeting with Lemass in 1965 was high stakes and he managed to annoy his colleagues by keeping them in the dark until Lemass was over the border. The central ideas – and they were low-key – were around cross-border co-operation in non-contentious areas such as electricity and tourism. But another crucial part of Lemass's agenda was improved economic relations with Britain; this had consequences for Northern Ireland and is another reminder that Northern Ireland could be easily treated differently from the rest of the UK. Lemass was frank about the interdependence of the British and Irish economies and the relevance of that to hoped-for EEC membership; central to adapting the economies was the dismantling of tariff barriers between the two countries. These sentiments culminated in the Anglo-Irish Free Trade Agreement signed in December 1965; that summer, in advance of the agreement, Lemass at a bilateral meeting with the British prime minister Harold Wilson proposed that under this agreement Ireland would be permitted to cut tariffs on Northern Irish goods sooner than for British goods which, though a surprise to Britain, was agreed to.[43]

There was no room, it appeared, for the airing of the base reality of northern nationalist subjugation in the midst of this 1960s 'dynamism' and economic liberalism, which was made apparent when an Irish television programme, *Radharc in Derry* (1964), focusing on the gerrymandering of local government, was not broadcast by RTÉ. Whether that was following political pressure is unclear, but it is hardly coincidental that the decision not to screen came as Lemass was preparing for détente with Terence O'Neill. Then controller of RTÉ, Gunnar Rugheimer, decided the programme was 'too sensitive' for transmission (the material highlighted what were to become key issues in the civil rights campaign a few years later).[44] It was not shown until 1989, and such censorship underlined the degree of partitionist thinking, part of what journalist Vincent Browne was later to lambast as 'a calculated, disguised indifference to the seething anger of a large part of the nationalist community'.[45]

The same year, a young Derry schoolteacher and former seminarian, John Hume, was asked by the *Irish Times*' editor, Douglas Gageby, to write articles on 'The Northern Catholic'. Hume was frank, not just about the shortcomings of the Nationalist Party in its inadequate responses ('nationalist politicians are prisoners of an image built up over forty years') but also the 'struggle for priority' between the desire to undo partition and confronting social and economic problems such as housing and unemployment: 'one gets the impression sometimes that the deep human problems which underlie the statistics are sometimes forgotten'. He also acknowledged the need to understand the unionist mindset and declared, 'Catholics should throw themselves fully into the solution of Northern problems.'[46] This was a lot more than southern nationalists had done. By the late 1960s, Catholics in Derry city comprised two-thirds of the population; in the 1967 local elections unionists duly won 32.1 per cent of the vote, but 60 per cent of the corporation seats.[47]

Legendary theatre director Tyrone Guthrie also dipped his toe into the border debate when he was chancellor of Queen's University Belfast from 1963 to 1970, provoking protest when, during a speech at Belfast City Hall, he described the border as wildly artificial and called on students to do their utmost to abolish it. He complained that his comments on that occasion were 'torn misleadingly from a much milder and more reasonable context', and that he did not expect to see the border abolished 'in our time'. Nor, he insisted, did he encourage students to 'fight' for its abolition but to 'work' for its gradual removal; he was concerned with the 'moral failure' to achieve human co-operation.[48]

As for the southern minority, by the end of the 1960s there were only 130,000 Protestants in the Republic; from 1946 to 1961 the Protestant population had fallen almost five times faster than the overall population. Master of the short story William Trevor dwelt on the psychological implications of that decline. Because of his preference for identifying with the outsider and his southern Protestant background he was well placed to creatively encapsulate the starkness of the decline, as seen in 'The Distant Past' (1979), where an Anglo-Irish brother and sister, the Middletons of Carraveagh, live in a decayed Georgian mansion sixty miles from the border. In the 1950s and 1960s they were seen as eccentrically quaint and Trevor used the telling phrase 'burnish of affection' to describe how the locals viewed them: 'On the day of the coronation of Queen Elizabeth II they drove into the town with a small Union Jack propped up in the back window of their

Ford Anglia.'[49] But as tensions increased in the late 1960s they impacted on the town, even tough it was some distance from the border ('over that distance had spread some wisps of the fogs of war'), and history and contemporary politics began to rear their divisive heads: 'On Fridays, only sometimes at first, there was a silence when the Middletons appeared. It was as though, going back nearly twenty years, people remembered the Union Jack in the window of their car and saw it now in a different light.'[50]

4

Violence and Containment

By 1969 the North was aflame and the border was once more in the spotlight in a contentious way. The emergence of the Troubles was due to a combination of failure to meet expectations about reform, militant Protestant backlash to talk of change, the civil rights movement championing nationalist grievances only to be brutally suppressed, British troops arriving in Northern Ireland 'in aid of the civil power', rioting at Catholic/Protestant interfaces, the beginning of the Provisional IRA's terrorist warfare and loyalist paramilitary retaliation. The endurance of the conflict over the subsequent three decades altered how the border question was framed with irredentist rhetoric, though not completely eschewed, ultimately superseded by a realisation that emotion needed to be replaced by reason.

Initially, however, the feeling generated by the violence created a sense in some quarters that the crisis could strengthen the prospects of a united Ireland. Some Irish diplomats foresaw Irish unity, but there was also acknowledgment of ignorance about northern unionists, and doubts about the wisdom of using the United Nations as a forum to highlight the growing crisis. Internal government documents show that, while it was recognised that the UN was unlikely to take action, it was important that the Irish government should be seen to be doing something for northern nationalists after the Irish external affairs (subsequently foreign affairs) minister Patrick Hillery, having been fobbed off by a junior minister in London citing the crisis as an internal UK matter, did not press the UN to bring the issue of intervention in Northern Ireland to a vote, 'since its rejection might be seen as copper fastening partition'.[1]

In November 1969, a memorandum from the Department of the Taoiseach reflecting on the outbreak of the Troubles had referred to southern Irish perceptions of the civil rights disturbances of the previous year. It was a time of heightened interest and awareness of the emergency in the North, but there was a suggestion that there could now also be a return to the lack of interest that had characterised southern attitudes to the North for decades. This was a position that had led to caustic remarks that the media and general public had only 'discovered' the North on 5 October 1968, when police had violently broken up a civil rights demonstration in Derry (the city, located beside the border, was a cockpit of the civil rights movement).[2] It was an observation that underlined ambivalence; Northern Ireland disturbances forced people in the Republic to think seriously about the border for the first time in decades, but there was no guarantee that such an interest would be maintained. Crisis engulfed Fianna Fáil, in power under Taoiseach Jack Lynch since 1966. Lynch responded hesitantly to the violence that Northern Ireland civil rights protestors were subjected to, but came under pressure from hawks in his own party, who sensed an opportunity to push the anti-partition agenda.

A controversial issue that emerged in 1969 was whether the government of the Republic was prepared to contemplate the sending of Irish troops over the border in response to the escalation of violence in Belfast and Derry. Lynch in 1969 sought to ride two horses; in March he spoke 'of seeking unity in Ireland by agreement between Irishmen' and abandoning all thought of using force 'as a means of undoing partition'. But he had not yet dispensed with his party's traditional anti-partitionism when addressing its national executive and he was under considerable internal pressure. On the night of 13 August he announced in a television address that the Irish government 'can no longer stand by and see innocent people injured and perhaps worse'; that it was establishing field hospitals along the border, and that it had asked the British government to seek the urgent dispatch of a UN peacekeeping force to Northern Ireland.

But a month previously, Patrick Hillery had asked, 'Where's the Northern Ireland desk?' at the end of his introductory tour of Iveagh House, the headquarters of his department, underlining the extent to which the Irish government was not remotely prepared for the Troubles.[3] Hillery was completely opposed to any intervention over the border, but Lynch's position was more ambiguous, despite claims to the contrary. A directive of February 1970 suggested a willingness to consider force, including cross-border incursions and the supply of arms and training for defensive purposes for northern nationalists (if security forces 'were unable and unwilling to protect the minority'); the directive was subsequently covered up and lies and evasions prevailed about its meanings and potential consequences.[4]

In January 1970 the speech made by Lynch to his party's annual gathering was plaintive:

> Partition is a deep, throbbing weal across the land, heart and soul of Ireland, an imposed deformity whose indefinite perpetuation eats into Irish consciousness like a cancer ... it is impossible for true Irishmen, of whatever creed, to dwell

on the existence of partition without becoming emotional. But emotionalism and the brand of impetuous action on demand that it leads to cannot possibly solve, or even help in dealing with, such a problem.[5]

There was a lot of exaggeration in this speech; 'true' Irishmen were well able to remain unemotional about the border by not engaging with it in any way; the festering sore remained quite abstract for most. True, younger activists were determined to start new campaigns, North and South; as Bernadette Devlin observed in relation to the 'Battle of the Bogside' in Derry, 'these people ... could never go back to the situation before August 12 1969'. But the references to the dangers of action driven by emotion was also an indication that Lynch was being increasingly influenced by T. K. Whitaker, the renowned former secretary of the Department of Finance, now governor of the central bank and a close confidant of Lynch.

Whitaker had been born in 1916 in Rostrevor, County Down before the creation of the border and moved with his family over that border when a child. In the fervid atmosphere generated by the Troubles he warned Lynch that 'emotion is a dangerous counsellor'. In 1969 he took control of Lynch's northern policy, wrote all his major speeches on this subject and proposed an all-Ireland federal authority. When Lynch gave a speech in Tralee in September 1969 affirming the commitment of the government 'to seek the reunification of the country by peaceful means' through agreement and as a long-term project, this was the work of Whitaker.[6] Whitaker was also friendly with Terence O'Neill, Northern Ireland's prime minister until 1969, and had encouraged and attended the historic meeting between O'Neill and Lemass in 1965 in Stormont. Whitaker urged 'seeking unity in Ireland by agreement between Irishmen' (there was simply 'no valid alternative' in his view) and abandonment of any idea of using force 'as a means of undoing partition'. He also believed it was futile to suggest Britain alone could solve this problem and desired to see Articles 2 and 3 of the Irish constitution, containing the territorial claim over Northern Ireland, scrapped. He also issued reminders of the gulf between the rhetoric of Irish unity versus the economic reality: Britain by 1970 was subsidising Northern Ireland to the tune of £100 million a year: 'We can't take over Britain's financial contributions, nor do we want the terrifying task of keeping sectarianism and anarchical mobs in order.'[7]

Lynch, however, was slow in moving against militants in his party. The arms crisis of 1970 caused a sensation when Lynch sacked two ministers, Neil Blaney and Charles Haughey, for not subscribing to party policy on Northern Ireland and a third, Kevin Boland, resigned in protest. Haughey was charged with importation of arms for use by northern nationalists and, though acquitted, the issue poisoned the politics of the period. Blaney had dismissed the view that unity could come only through consent, maintaining that the use of force should not be ruled out. With Haughey, he secured the establishment of a cabinet subcommittee on Northern Ireland which, it was often subsequently argued, deliberately kept other cabinet members in the dark.

Most controversially, the two became involved in schemes to supply arms to Catholic self-defence groups in the North (largely fronts for the Provisional IRA) in association with the military intelligence officer Captain James Kelly, who claimed – convincingly, given recent private discussions of possible assistance, including military, over the border – that he was acting with the approval of the government.[8] Haughey was also attempting to gain political advantage by cashing in on heightened outrage; southern Irish opinion at this point may have included 'a significant sneaking admiration for those prepared to take risks for Northern nationalists', but the predominant sentiment saw the stability of the Irish state as a greater value.[9]

Kevin Boland created a rival republican party, Aontacht Éireann; it soon floundered, and he complained, 'The people didn't want a republican party'. Fianna Fáil had clearly been unprepared for the outbreak of the Troubles, but by 1971 it had settled on certain things, including a new engagement with constitutional nationalists in the North – which represented a historic shift – and the dispelling of the suggestion that violence was legitimate in pursuit of a united Ireland.[10] But Boland's point regarding the lack of interest in a republican party was well made; Aontacht Éireann ran thirteen candidates in the 1973 general election and all were defeated; the party expired three years later.

Catholics from Northern Ireland had poured over the border into the Republic from 1969 to 1972; they were officially described in the Republic as 'refugees from strife-torn Northern Ireland'; many were housed in cold, primitive huts with no running water. The description of them as refugees faded, as did public consciousness of them. There are no reliable statistics, but it has been estimated that up to 11,000 people were displaced; on a single day in August 1971 in Belfast there were an estimated 1,000 homeless because of sectarian violence and by the early twenty-first century there were 22,290 North-born people living in the southern border counties of Monaghan, Louth and Donegal.[11]

As to the response of British politicians during these heady Irish days, historian Jonathan Bardon has suggested, 'Having kept themselves in a woeful state of ignorance for so long, Westminster governments had to take a crash course in an attempt to understand the intricacies of the Northern Ireland imbroglio. For three fateful years they hesitated to invoke the 1920 act and impose direct rule'.[12] Assertions of such profound British ignorance have been challenged; the three prime ministers who had to deal with the problem in this era – Harold Wilson, Ted Heath and James Callaghan – had all visited Northern Ireland before the Troubles. But brief pleasure or business trips hardly amounted to deep engagement. As Paul Bew sees it, the problem was not so much blindness as a tendency to see Northern Ireland through the prism of the 1920s ('which scarred so many politicians') or more recently, its contribution to the Second World War effort. While the Foreign Office submitted 'a rather theoretical paper' on British withdrawal, Callaghan as home secretary dismissed it and, revealingly, 'nobody understood the finances of Northern Ireland' which Sir Richard Hopkins, Treasury controller in 1939, had memorably described as 'fudges, dodges and wangles'; massive intervention had been needed to preserve parity with the rest of the UK.[13]

At least with the outbreak of the Troubles, for some British MPs Northern Ireland was no longer abstract: Labour MP Stan Orme was in Derry and 'saw for myself the B Specials [a division of the RUC justifiably seen by Catholics as serving unionist interests] firing gas into the Bogside ... I have never been so frightened in my life.'[14] But there was no excuse for much of the innocence; Denis Healey, for example, defence secretary at the outbreak of the Troubles, found himself walking the streets of a Belfast he knew nothing about, despite the fact that his paternal grandfather was Irish: 'It was, surprisingly, my first visit to the land of my fathers ... again and again I recalled the undergraduate debate on Ulster which I heard at Balliol [Oxford] and my fatal ignorance when my father stumped me by asking for the Labour Party's policy on Irish unity in the 1945 election campaign.'[15] He had not done much homework in the meantime and there was no originality or insight guiding his thinking on the Ulster question.

The Troubles prompted the formation of new political organisations including the nationalist Social and Democratic Labour

Party (SDLP) in 1970 and, the following year, the Democratic Unionist Party (DUP), founded by Ian Paisley and Desmond Boal as a successor to the Protestant Unionist Party and opposed to any reformist unionism. The creation of the SDLP ensured a steady traffic of northern nationalists in the direction of Dublin. Infighting, distrust and class tensions pervaded the SDLP, of which John Hume was a co-founder and deputy leader, eventually taking over the leadership from Gerry Fitt in 1979. Fitt did not share the enthusiasm the university-educated Hume and his other colleagues had for position papers, drafting, redrafting and engaging with politicians south of the border; he saw them more as committed nationalists than social democrats.

In any case, as far as senior officials and politicians in Dublin were concerned, it was Hume rather than Fitt who was the real nationalist leader in Northern Ireland. Eamonn Gallagher, for example, the senior Irish government official working in liaison with northern nationalist politicians, became a close confidant of Hume, and as early as July 1971 he noted that the Irish government recognised Hume as 'the real leader of the non-unionists in the North'. Leading SDLP members, including Hume and Paddy Devlin, had cultivated contacts in the South and sought to raise awareness and funds there, though they also had to assure Fianna Fáil that the SDLP was not seeking to encroach on southern electoral territory. But Hume's trips to Dublin were often politically fraught; there was some wariness of his idea of joint administration of Northern Ireland by the British and Irish governments, and his rejection of the assertion that 'even mentioning Irish unity was to risk civil war'.[16]

Other events over the next few years – most notoriously Bloody Sunday in January 1972, when thirteen unarmed protestors were shot dead in Derry by British paratroopers – again acutely focused southern attention on Northern Ireland, but what also became clear as the decade progressed was that, whatever about the anger of the South in relation to the Troubles, there was also a concerted political determination to ensure that the Troubles were contained in Northern Ireland and would not spill over the border.

This ensured that any heightened sense of all-Ireland nationalist sentiment and anger was relatively quickly qualified. Eamonn McCann, one of the original organisers of the Northern Ireland Civil Rights Association (NICRA) and a participant in the disturbances in Derry from the late 1960s, later reflected on the degree to which Bloody Sunday was an event that ultimately helped to reconcile the Republic to partition. The immediate aftermath of the killings witnessed mass protests, and the burning of the British embassy in Dublin, and never before or since has there been 'a sense in the South of oneness with the North'. But there was also, at the political and military level, nervousness about the course this sentiment might take. Within days, the insistence on preserving the institutions of the state, bolstering its policing and security and stamping out the menace of 'anarchists', characterised the political rhetoric. In the words of journalist John Healy, who wrote on politics for the *Irish Times*, senior Fianna Fáil politicians' rhetoric created 'the feeling that the North is nothing more than a functional historical claim: a thing so long reduced to standard clichés like our fourth green field that it isn't real any more'. There was a clear emotional and intellectual disengagement from the North.[17]

Anglo-Irish summits inevitably became tense affairs between Ted Heath and Jack Lynch. In 1969 Heath had sought out Erskine Childers, then Irish deputy prime minister, at a London reception, and hectored him for the audacity of the Irish government in interfering in Northern Ireland. Heath also, in effect, threatened economic sanctions against the Republic by revisiting the terms of the Anglo-Irish Free Trade Agreement. In 1971 John Peck, the British ambassador in Dublin, was distinctly unimpressed with Heath, later characterising one of his meetings with Lynch as a 'dialogue of the deaf'. Lynch complained of the 'waning' of the Irish government's influence in the North because of internment of suspects without trial, introduced in August 1971. While Heath accepted that reunification was 'a rightful aspiration to hold', stating that 'if at some future date the majority of people in Northern Ireland want unification and express that desire in the appropriate constitutional manner, I do not believe any British government would stand in their way', he was 'not prepared to tell others what they ought to want ... where Ireland is unrealistic is in thinking that one million unionists want a united Ireland', though he made it clear he had no regard for Ian Paisley.[18]

After Bloody Sunday there was a realisation that events were spiralling out of control, and on 24 March 1972 Heath announced that London would immediately prorogue Stormont and assume direct responsibility for the administration of Northern Ireland, which was widely regarded as undermining the Union. Later that year Lynch argued that, 'when the British army is not successful sealing the border from their side, then the Republic cannot be expected to be', given its much smaller military strength; Lynch also wondered whether the border question could be approached as a regional issue in the context of the EEC 'without regard to the border itself'.[19]

Amidst the flurry, it was not the case that Irish politicians detected a burning southern passion for Irish unity. In 1972 John Peck reported that he had asked Lynch how important the issue of reunification was to the republic's electorate, and 'his answer amounted to saying that they could not care less. As far as he was concerned, he wanted peace and justice in the North and close friendship and co-operation with us'.[20] Over subsequent decades, a version of that solution was eventually arrived at but it was a tortuous and bloody journey and the border was the subject of much policing, security and accusations of bad faith.

Privately, after the enormity of Bloody Sunday, Sir Alec Douglas-Home, the British foreign secretary, was pessimistic about finding a framework that would keep Northern Ireland in the UK and saw a united Ireland as a long-term solution. Heath, however, preferred to emphasise the failure of the Republic to stem IRA attacks in Northern Ireland; he was prepared to make some sympathetic grunts about the idea, pushed by Lynch, of a Council of Ireland, but in a common market, social and economic context, and he would not commit to negotiations on it. What preoccupied the Irish side was the idea of a Council of Ireland with 'the possibility of evolution'. Heath was being nudged along and Lynch was making progress; nor was Heath the friend Ulster Unionists hoped; as historian Joe Lee characterised it, he had 'no intention of placing Britain in moral bondage to Ulster Unionism'.[21]

Nonetheless, ten years later on a visit to Belfast, Heath described himself as 'the best friend Ulster ever had'.[22] It was more likely he had a wariness and dislike of both sides. Heath had ordered, in the event of the British government losing control, contingency plans which included the redrawing of the border to transfer large sections of the population and an influx of British troops 'to swamp all extremist strongholds' on both sides, a proposal never implemented, but Heath did oversee the authorisation of the phrase the 'Irish dimension'; the recognition that Dublin had to be part of the solution.[23]

Greater engagement with the problem of Northern Ireland also came during a period when Britain's international status, prestige and economic power were in decline and it needed to rethink its alliances, foreign-policy priorities and involvement in Europe.

Reference to increased European integration as providing a possibility for improved relations between Britain and Ireland and
within Northern Ireland worked their way in to 'The Future of
Northern Ireland', a green paper published by the British government in November 1972, which stated, 'It is clearly desirable that
any new arrangement, while meeting the wishes of Northern Ireland and Great Britain be so far as possible acceptable by the Republic of Ireland which from January first 1973 will share the rights and
obligations of membership of the European Community.'[24]

Both Britain and Ireland duly joined the EEC on that same
day in 1973. Taoiseach Seán Lemass had been adamant in 1962
that with eventual membership of a common market 'partition
will become so obviously an anachronism that all sensible people
will want to bring it to an end'. Seán Kennan, the Irish ambassador
to Europe, was optimistic a decade later that 'membership would
obviously contribute significantly towards the ending of partition',
while Patrick Hillery, as minister for foreign affairs, declared that
'Northern Ireland will become a European problem'.[25] In truth,
the EEC (later EU) stayed largely aloof from the Troubles.

Nor did membership of the EEC initially see free trade in
agricultural produce, and the Common Agricultural Policy 'created major incentives' for smuggling between North and South:
'In 1977 an estimated 5,000 pigs a week crossed the border ille-
gally; some appear to have made several journeys.' The eventual
introduction of the single market in 1993 brought an end to that.[26]
On a tour of the border decades later, Garrett Carr was told that
during the era of inventive smuggling, thirty bottles of spirits
could be contained in the carcass of a cow being moved from the
knacker's yard over the border, while diesel smuggling eventually
became 'an industry' when it was cheaper in the South, and some
of the filtering processes involved in clearing the smuggled fuel of
its dye were on a grand scale.[27]

A border poll was conducted in March 1973; the Conservative government had intended that such a poll would be held every ten years, but it was largely boycotted by Catholics and a 'meaningless majority of more than 500,000 backed the status quo'. On the day of the poll there were five explosions in Derry and six in Belfast, where a British sentry was also killed. One estimate from Derry was that only 1 per cent of Catholics voted in their areas.[28] Fourteen men from an interparty delegation from Westminster toured polling booths and there were allegations of impersonation and malpractice. As Journalist Walter Ellis noted wryly, 'Up the Falls Road [in Belfast] Catholics studiously ignored the whole affair and carried on their normal business with scarcely a sideways glance at the official stations supplied liberally by a democratic England ... the Shankhill, however, burgeoned with determined Loyalists; they littered the street and their flags were a riot of British and Ulster hues.'[29]

The result was entirely predictable. As Gerry Fitt of the SDLP was to note, it indicated nothing that was not already known: that there were more Protestants and unionists than nationalists and Catholics in Northern Ireland. The NICRA lashed out at Willie Whitelaw, secretary of state for Northern Ireland, for trying to make the border an issue in politics when the real issue should have been democratic rights. Of the total Northern Ireland electorate of 1,035,000, 59 per cent cast ballots with 591,820 voting to retain the UK link and 6,463, or 0.62 per cent, voting against. About 90 per cent of the unionist population had come out to support the Union. Eddie McAteer, the leader of the Nationalist Party who had advocated a boycott of the poll, suggested the result 'will surely settle the Irish border problem for another ten minutes or so'. McAteer had long maintained that only a slow constitutional approach by nationalists would lead to unification, but by now he was on the way out, squeezed by the SDLP and having been burnt by a civil rights momentum that he regarded as too 'six-county orientated', which meant a downgrading of the border question and an annoyance at the determination of John Hume and others to demand 'British Rights for British subjects'.

The same month, a British government white paper proposed an eighty-member elected assembly for Northern Ireland and a devolved cross-community (power-sharing) government. It further proposed that control of security matters would remain with Westminster, and that provision be made for the setting up of a Council of Ireland for North–South discussion on relevant matters. Northern Ireland Prime Minister Brian Faulkner cautiously welcomed the paper as a basis for discussion, but the proposed Council of Ireland was contentious and needed to be agreed on a tripartite basis among the governments of Britain, Northern Ireland and the Republic, which was now governed by a Fine Gael/Labour coalition under the premiership of Liam Cosgrave. Faulkner felt he could limit the competence of the Council of Ireland to peripheral policy matters, securing a pledge from the Irish government accepting that 'there could be no change in the status of Northern Ireland until a majority' desired it, and setting in train cross-border security initiatives.

These proposals ultimately led to the Sunningdale Agreement, but as well as general unionist nervousness, DUP fulminating and republican scorn, there were also fault lines within northern nationalism and the SDLP was not always a united party when it came to dealing with southern governments. It did not help that Conor Cruise O'Brien was a minister in the Republic from 1973 to 1977 and was now ideologically far removed from his younger self, when he had worked on the Republic's anti-partition crusade in the 1950s. What he now referred to was the 'national fantasy' in relation to partition:

The present writer blushes to recall that at one time he devoted a considerable part of his professional activity, as a member of the Department of External Affairs, to what was known as 'anti-partition'. The only positive result of the activity, as far as I was concerned, was that it led me to discover the cavernous inanities of 'anti-partition' and of government propaganda generally.[30]

In his book *States of Ireland* (1972) he maintained the Irish Catholic community had 'an infatuation with its own mythology' and criticised the Republic's 'colonial claim' on the North.[31] This was a toxic revisionism that amounted to unionism as far as his critics, including John Hume, were concerned; Hume regarded it as 'the most subtle defence of unionism which has yet appeared'.[32]

O'Brien continually fired off missives to Taoiseach Liam Cosgrave and his minister for foreign affairs, Garret FitzGerald, and rejected the idea of a Council of Ireland; FitzGerald, in turn, dismissed his rebuff. Meanwhile, there was a concern within the British government that FitzGerald was 'too much under the influence of Hume in relation to Northern Ireland matters'.[33] The SDLP feared it would be 'sold down the river' if it agreed to power sharing before settling on the 'Irish dimension'.[34] The SDLP had little trust in Dublin, despite visits to Dublin providing a welcome release from the tension and violence of the North and the boozy hospitality that came with such visits. Nor were SDLP members such as Paddy Devlin shy in making their views known, to the extent that Cosgrave drafted a letter to Fitt complaining of 'your party's attitude to my government'.[35]

One real sticking point was that the SDLP believed that a Council of Ireland should have jurisdiction over policing matters in Northern Ireland and that in the border area, both southern and northern police forces could work in conjunction, but as the

Irish government saw it there were constitutional complications in giving such a council control over the Gardaí (southern police), so interim measures were needed. Irish Diplomat Seán Donlon met with SDLP members in October 1973 and they claimed Dublin 'is not with them on policing'. They went as far as to describe the government's attitude as 'generally partitionist' and indicated that 'Dublin may not be sincere in its approach to Irish unity'. They also, in an assertion that would have enraged the government, threatened 'to turn quickly to Fianna Fáil with hope of getting their support on the policing question'.[36]

Nonetheless, agreement was reached in December 1973. As a settlement designed to bridge nationalist and unionist aspirations, the Sunningdale Agreement remained the prototype, but it abjectly failed at this juncture due to militant unionist and loyalist opposition and was not formally ratified. It also exposed deficiencies in the Irish and British governments' approaches. In the view of Garret FitzGerald (who maintained that Articles 2 and 3 of the Irish constitution containing the territorial claim over Northern Ireland were of 'no practical value'), 'I pushed too far for too much' in relation to a Council of Ireland, while in the view of Cosgrave, the fault was with Britain as Harold Wilson did not have the bottle to stand up to the 'mobs' that brought down the power-sharing assembly in May 1974; he believed a Conservative government would have stood firm.[37]

For the government of the Republic, the Sunningdale balancing act was further complicated and compromised when former Fianna Fáil minister Kevin Boland took a legal challenge to the agreement on the grounds that the Irish government's support of it amounted to recognition of Northern Ireland, thus violating the Irish constitution. This was rejected by the High Court but the government's defence 'amounted to a declaration that its territorial claim to Northern Ireland was still in force', which enraged

Faulkner as it 'robbed him of all credibility on the question of status'. This was later acknowledged by FitzGerald, who conceded to a unionist that 'our legal defence involved demolishing the entire political position which we had built up for you'.[38]

In 1974 came the sensational murder of a young farmer and Fine Gael senator, Billy Fox, by the IRA. Ironically, Fox was sympathetic to republicanism; he was killed by a thirteen-member IRA gang who were raiding the home of his fiancée near Clones. The death of a member of Parliament in a blatantly sectarian killing caused outrage and reinforced the fears (widely shared in official Dublin circles in the early and mid 1970s) that the Northern Ireland conflict might destabilise the Republic; however, Fox was the only member of the Oireachtas killed during the Troubles. As historian Patrick Maume characterised it, 'Fox's career reflected both the increasing political integration of a new generation of border Protestants within the republic's political system and the persistence of sectarian divisions and whispered hatreds along the border.'[39]

Such enmity also impacted on writers. In the early 1970s poet Seamus Heaney, born in County Derry to a Catholic family in 1939, moved over the border to live in the Republic in order to concentrate on his art. He faced an interesting dilemma; or, as he put it in 1972, he experienced, a 'pull in two directions, back through the political and cultural trauma of Ireland and out towards the urgencies and experience of the world beyond it'. At school he studied both the Gaelic literature of Ireland as well as English literature, and 'since then I have maintained a notion of myself as Irish in a province that insists it is British. Lately I realised that these complex pieties and dilemmas were implicit in the very terrain where I was born.'[40] This was about the split culture of Ulster, or in the metaphor of his poem 'Terminus':

Two buckets were easier carried than one.
I grew up in between.[41]

Writing for himself, over the border, did carry a degree of
guilt about abandonment, but if he had become a 'political' poet
this would have come at great expense. Heaney did not ignore the
Troubles or the border; to a certain extent he floated above them,
observing from a distance, but he did not elide the feelings generated by the border checks and a subjugated, suspected, scrutinised
people, seen in *From the Frontier of Writing*:

> The tightness and the nilness round that space
> when the car stops in the road, the troops inspect
> its make and number and, as one bends his face
> towards your window, you catch sight of more
> on a hill beyond, eyeing with intent
> down cradled guns that hold you under cover.[42]

Politicians also felt they were being pulled in two directions.
In replacing Heath as British prime minister in 1974, Harold Wilson had to confront what he referred to as 'the division of Ireland
and its resultant centuries of misery'.[43] In November 1971, with
'Mr Heath's approval and help', Wilson had travelled to Northern
Ireland and the Republic for a series of meetings and then put forward his programme to tackle the problem; cessation of violence,
interparty talks leading to tripartite discussions 'aimed at establishing a constitutional commission of the three governments to
examine the implications of a united Ireland with protection for
minorities, north and south'. Also envisaged was possible membership of the Commonwealth for the Republic, with 'guaranteed social service provisions for Northern Ireland citizens they
had enjoyed in the UK'. Wilson later acknowledged that this

fifteen-year plan was 'not realistic'. What transpired instead was the power-sharing executive, which did not work, maintained Wilson, because 'intimidation became virtually total'.[44]

Wilson then threw fuel on the fire by making his 'spongers' broadcast; given that the British state was spending £300 million annually on Northern Ireland,

> with the cost of army operations on top of that ... they see property destroyed by evil violence and are asked to pick up the bill for rebuilding it ... yet people who benefit from this now viciously defy Westminster ... spend their lives *sponging* on Westminster and British democracy and then systematically assault democratic methods.[45]

Poor Harold's holiday in the Isles of Scilly had to be cut short due to the resultant furore and the deteriorating situation in Belfast. Having been burnt, it was no wonder he concluded, 'no solution could be imposed from across the water. From now on we had to throw the task clearly to the Northern Ireland people themselves.'[46]

Merlyn Rees, secretary of state for Northern Ireland from 1974 to 1976, echoed the idea that the British government 'could only hold the ring to make it possible for a solution to be worked out'. He was privately scathing about commentators who maintained that a speedy resolution might be brought about by some grand constitutional initiative imposed from above. Rees believed devolution with power sharing must remain the long-term objective, and integrationism (the view that the province should be permanently integrated into the UK) should be firmly ruled out. But he also advised the cabinet that Northern Ireland politicians were not capable of running the province as those with government experience had mostly left public life and the new ones were protest politicians unprepared to wield power.[47]

That sense of hopelessness and drift had a significant impact on the SDLP. In his reports of the situation in Northern Ireland in the spring of 1974 Seán Donlon witnessed 'depression, frustration and despair' and 'much bickering' within the SDLP. John Hume and Austin Currie 'seem to feel that the SDLP is finished as a political force'. Hume was stark in his assessment: 'Any hope of Irish unity has gone forever.' It was a reminder that although Hume was associated with a conciliatory approach towards unionists, he retained his strongly nationalist perspective.[48]

This despondency in the aftermath of the failed power-sharing experiment led Hume to look outside Ireland, and his meetings and perseverance paid off. He went to the US because, in SDLP colleague Séamus Mallon's words, 'quite simply ... there was nowhere else to go'. A statement from the US president Jimmy Carter in August 1977 was seen by some as an initiative that 'fell flat' in Ireland, although it was regarded as breaking half a century of silence by the White House on Northern Ireland. It committed the US to supporting power sharing and averred that the US had an interest in a settlement.[49] Hume was disappointed with Dublin's response; indeed, Hume was often disappointed with Dublin's responses and his prickly stubbornness and sensitivity to criticism irked others, including those who did not accept that Hume's commitment to the consent principle in relation to Northern Ireland's future was compatible with his suggestion that Britain abandon its guarantee to Northern Ireland. Fianna Fáil sought to develop this idea by preparing a joint Fianna Fáil/SDLP strategy around it, but Hume evaded the trap of being tied to or enveloped by one political party in the South.

Another interesting character who elaborated on the border was diplomat John Peck; independent of mind and keen to become historically literate about Ireland following his appointment as British ambassador in April 1970, he insisted Britain needed to recognise the 'Irish dimension' to the border problem. Peck was not typical; he had an exceptional affinity with Ireland, was sympathetic to Irish nationalism and lived out the rest of his life in Dublin after retirement in 1973.

He noted that 'people talk and act as if the border were something as impenetrable and controllable as the Berlin Wall', but, as he pointed out, the border 'is not actually visible … 1970/1 was the first time that it actually mattered whether the border ran one side of a ditch or the other or whether a culvert was British or Irish sovereign territory'. With the blocking of border-crossing roads by blowing craters in them and closing them with large spikes set in concrete, 'the village priest, the doctor, the farmer and the vet might have to make considerable detours to go about their normal business'.[50] Darach MacDonald, who grew up in Clones, County Monaghan and became a professional journalist in the 1970s, recalled that Clones had been a prosperous market town and rail hub devastated by partition ('teetering on the brink of ruin') and told how his childhood landscape was affected:

> I was a toddler when steel girders were driven deep through the road's surface at the Aqueduct Bridge at the edge of Clones; the spikes circumscribed my childhood world in a ring of steel … my uncle's [writer Eugene McCabe] farm was cut off when the road was spiked by the border. He built a small link road through a corner of a field so that he could get to town.[51]

This was a reminder that not all accepted these impositions without a fight, and such defiance included the filling in of craters to prevent the inconvenience of longer road journeys (in one case a thirty-mile detour as opposed to five miles direct). Both unionists and nationalists were inconvenienced by road closures when it came to commercial and social connections.[52] Watchtowers also became part of the border landscape, because the border was of such strategic importance to the IRA, especially in South Armagh; as Garrett Carr reminisced, 'from everywhere in South Armagh you could see a tower and a tower could see you ... the towers gave South Armagh the feeling of an open prison.'[53] During the Troubles in Armagh, 468 people were killed; a small, angry, seventy-five-year-old woman, Margaret Frazer in South Armagh, whose husband and brother and brother-in-law were killed by the IRA, told journalist Susan McKay for her seminal book *Northern Protestants: An Unsettled People* (2000): 'I come from Kangaroo country ... it was your own neighbours was trying to burn you out.'[54]

For some of those enduring the daily stress of the Troubles, the Republic, in contrast, seemed somewhat idyllic; in March 1978 a resident of Derry, who had an unemployed husband and young children, wrote of occasional day trips across the border: 'once I get over that border checkpoint I feel free as a bird. No soldiers or searches or bombed empty spaces where once shops and homes, dances and cinemas used to be. It's lovely.'[55] For those children travelling in the opposite direction as day trippers, crossing the border, after the often tortuous delays at checkpoints and the shock of being so close to young British soldiers bearing arms, was a 'gateway to this excitement' of better sweets and greater choice of 'biscuits, toys – everything important.'[56] But the partition mentality remained strong in the South and many who moved over the border from the North for longer stretches felt this deeply; there was ignorance but also a guarded and sometimes hostile attitude towards the 'Nordies'. Poet John Montague, who studied at UCD, suggested 'the North of Ireland from which I emerged was barely comprehensible to my Southern contemporaries.'[57] Derry socialist and feminist Nell McCafferty, who became a well-known journalist in Dublin, surmised that 'Northerners were not always welcome in Southern society. Our accent alone marked us out, and our rapid-fire way of talking was associated with war.'[58] Susan McKay, who grew up as a Protestant in Derry and came to Trinity College Dublin in 1975, referred to the 'strange silences' on the part of those who had lived through the early years of the Troubles and then moved to Dublin, but she also felt that 'many in the Republic were oblivious.'[59]

Others found themselves negotiating the border for social reasons or as part of campaigns for increased individual rights. Northern Ireland was no beacon of liberality; another indication of it being different from the rest of the UK was that the 1967 Abortion Act was not extended there, but there was more contraception available than in the Republic, where artificial birth control had been banned since 1935. Frank Crummey, a founding member of the Fertility Guidance Clinic opened in Dublin in 1969, was part of a group that set up a company to import contraceptives in bulk and it was his job to smuggle them over the border: '"We had some great fun", he recalled: "One day I was stopped in Balbriggan by these Gardaí doing an arms check. I had 40,000 French letters in the station wagon and insisted they were all for my own personal use." "Ah go *way*," they said finally.'[60]

Members of the Irish Women's Liberation Movement also traversed the border on a train in search of contraceptives in May 1971 in a publicity stunt, and on their return, dared the Irish customs officers to arrest them. The defiance, however, masked a certain ignorance on the part of some of the women; they didn't have prescriptions for contraceptive pills and weren't aware these were needed. As Nell McCafferty recalled, 'I did not fancy us returning to Dublin armed only with condoms, which would have concentrated the mind of the nation on male nether regions; on sex; on anything but birth control. Unthinkable. So I bought hundreds of packets of aspirin.' The wrapping was taken off them before the train reached Dublin and when faced with the customs officers the women announced, "'These are birth control pills and we are taking them and you are not getting them.'"[61]

More bleakly, John Peck and others also frequently maintained that the area south of the border 'became one vast safe haven for gunmen on the run from the North, for IRA training camps and operational bases'.[62] This was contested; as Taoiseach, Liam Cosgrave robustly defended the record of Irish governments in this regard, highlighting in March 1974, for example, that in the previous year 208 people had been brought to trial by the Special Criminal Court in Dublin in relation to terrorist activities; he also pointed out that the strength of the Gardaí had been increased by 500 'and is now at its highest since the foundation of the state'. In 1973, 6,500 border controls and '16,500 joint Garda/ army road check points were set up'.[63]

Four years later, Cosgrave and his ministers were more specific in relation to the question of violence being directed from the Republic and insisted

> by far the greatest proportion of violence in Northern Ireland is indigenous. In fact, of all incidents of violence there, only 2 per cent have any connection with the border ... it is notable that in Northern Ireland where the security forces are more numerous than in the Republic and are patrolling an area one-third its size it has been found difficult to contain the violence occurring there. This is not said in any spirit of triumphalism.[64]

But there was also the question of what constituted an illegal excursion over the border. John Peck had to deal with 'a bundle of complaints, regrets, promises to investigate, requests for information. A British armoured car had invaded Irish sovereign territory. A helicopter had violated Irish air space. Irish villages had filled in a crater in Northern Ireland. It isn't in Northern Ireland. It is. It isn't.'[65] There was co-operation between the RUC, the British army and the Gardaí throughout the 1970s; the co-operation has been described as 'discreet', which meant officially it did not happen or was just coincidental; or, as Patrick Mulroe has described it, 'the difficulty for the Irish state was not so much in co-operating with the British state but being seen to co-operate' throughout a time when vicious tit-for-tat killings were a regular occurrence in the border area.[66]

The Irish state also had a preoccupation with keeping the conflict 'contained' in Northern Ireland, which was never fully possible; Patrick Mulroe instances, for example a two-hour gun battle across the Armagh–Louth border at Dungooley in January 1972 during which the British army fired 2,500 rounds at the IRA on the southern side, all the while being observed by Irish army and police, but there were no arrests made.[67]

The Miami Showband massacre illustrated the truly awful scale of border brutality in 1975 as loyalist paramilitaries impersonated security forces; the band members were returning over the border after performing in Banbridge, County Down. One of Ireland's leading bands at the time, their music and line-up transcended the border; as Stephen Travers, one of the survivors, was later to recall, 'We had no interest in politics, we just wanted to play music.' Three of the band members were summarily executed and collusion between agents of the British state and the loyalist paramilitaries was suspected, as it was in other cases; thirty-five years after the showband killings evidence of official collusion between the killers and members of the Ulster Defence Regiment, a regiment of the British army, was presented publicly. In relation to the Dublin/Monaghan bombings of 17 May 1974, orchestrated by the Ulster Volunteer Force, which killed thirty-three people, thus making it the deadliest single day during the Troubles, there was a 'shameful failure' to track down the perpetrators of the bombings, the strong likelihood that the bombers received assistance, and accusations that some Gardaí were wittingly or unwittingly working for the British.[68]

Along with musical endeavours, sport could also transcend the border, but not without complications, and not all sports could manage it. Inevitably, the border had implications for many sporting and recreational impulses. Those organising cock-fighting, seen by many as a sport, were driven to more and more remote places and the border was useful to evade law enforcers on both sides; if rumbled on one side there could be a 'frantic stampede' to the other, and there were many 'good humoured tales of evasion and derring-do'.[69] Sports historian Paul Rouse observes that those involved in organising soccer in Ireland were embroiled in the conflict that led to partition, resulting in two associations vying to control the sport there. Soccer was thus profoundly impacted by the 'mutual suspicion' between Dublin and Belfast; sporting change and greater organisation coincided with political upheaval and 'this played a major role in shaping modern Irish sport and in ensuring that sport in Ireland held characteristics shared by no other country'. While the new sporting world was 'capable of transcending Ireland's political, economic, social and cultural divides, it had also shown itself capable of underlining – even aggravating – such divides'.[70]

The Irish Football Association (IFA), dominated by Belfast-based administrators, had initially controlled Irish soccer competitions, but in September 1921, as a consequence of partition, a rival, southern-based Football Association of Ireland (FAI) was established. Achieving international recognition for the two was tortuous; internationally, both fielded teams known as 'Ireland'

and both freely chose players from both sides of the border. A reflection of the absurdity was that in February 1946, Manchester United captain Johnny Carey played for the IFA team against England and then did the same for the FAI team two days later. Eventually, the IFA fielded its team as Northern Ireland and the FAI fielded theirs as the Republic of Ireland, and players now had to play for one or the other: 'amidst this agreement, the idea of fielding a single team to represent Ireland remained unattainable'.[71]

The situation with rugby was different as those who controlled it sought to place it outside of partition. Since the 1880s rugby had been organised on a provincial structure; the team continued to straddle the new border but there were dilemmas for the Irish Rugby Football Union regarding which side of the border should it play its internationals and in relation to flags, emblems and anthems. The jersey and the emblem did not change and home matches were split between Dublin and Belfast. There were continuing controversies about flags (it was agreed in 1932 that the tricolour would fly alongside the IRFU flag at international matches in Dublin) but the IRFU managed a 'fine balancing act' amidst continuing tetchiness in the 1930s about a toast to the King of England at IRFU dinners; as Rouse characterises it 'there may have been moments of discomfort, but none so great that compromise could not be secured'.[72]

The Gaelic Athletic Association (GAA) in existence since 1884 as an organisation to promote Gaelic football and hurling, also continued to organise on an all-Ireland basis, but that did not make it cross-community; the GAA banned from membership anyone who played rugby, soccer, cricket or hockey, or attended these games, and vigilante committees kept tabs. Members of the police, the British army, the navy and and prison services were also banned. The ban in relation to other sports was rescinded in

1971 but the prohibition on British security forces membership remained until 2001.[73]

The Crossmaglen GAA club in South Armagh became the centre of attention because of the security that developed around it when the expansion of the police base in the town led to the requisition of a large part of the GAA's grounds and property, and 'claim and counterclaim followed for the best part of three decades' before the club grounds were returned to the club in 1999.[74] This sense of siege and persecution allowed a particular identity to develop, one based not only on resentment at the British security presence but also on a sense of abandonment by the GAA, and 'this belief helped develop an edge to the character of border people not obvious elsewhere in Ireland ... people in the area thought that the GAA's central administration should have addressed the issue more frequently and more rigorously' (not irrelevant was the fact that the GAA also accepted significant funding from the British state).

This was part of a wider experience of sport around the Irish border region, enabling those living there 'to express an added dimension to their political beliefs and aspirations', but it also complicated the issue of the GAA and politicisation.[75] It also engendered resentment about those south of the border, and therein lay the conundrum of nationalists along the border who aspired towards a united Ireland and did their bit to promote Irish sporting and cultural identity yet who were also protective of their 'independence' and perhaps put that distinctiveness ahead of Irish unity. Irish sports journalist Joe Pilkington summed it up well in characterising these as people who 'never classed themselves as northerners. They never really wanted to be southerners either. They were a semi-state on their own', reconciled to neither the northern nor southern state.[76]

5

Kinks, Wiggles and Diplomacy

How did the border question fare in the 1980s? There was a need, historian Ronan Fanning noted wryly during that decade, to confront British-Irish realities: 'Britain looms larger in the Irish consciousness than Ireland in the British; this has always been and will remain, among the most significant of these realities'; he underlined 'the perennial difficulty of commanding British attention'.[1] With Margaret Thatcher's ascension to Downing Street this serious challenge endured, though there were initially some encouraging signals. In 1980, Thatcher and new Fianna Fáil Taoiseach Charles Haughey agreed to develop not just 'new and closer political co-operation between their two governments' but also the commissioning of joint studies to consider the 'totality of relationships within these islands'.[2] Haughey, who had declared on taking office that his priority was to end partition by agreement with the British government, exaggerated what this amounted to for a domestic and US audience, implying that the British government was willing to contemplate the end of partition soon, and Anglo-Irish relations cooled. But just how serious was Haughey about ending partition? He acidly referred to Northern Ireland in 1980 as a 'failed political entity' and the border in 1986 as 'economic, social and geographic nonsense'.[3]

But was it a political nonsense? Was there a political solution to the challenge it represented? And did southern Ireland really care that much, given its preoccupation with its devastated economy? Haughey was well aware that much of the southern electorate was uninterested and that Northern Ireland was a 'footnote' rather than a mainstay of general election campaigns. Nor could he persuade US president Ronald Reagan to play the green card in Washington, a miffed Haughey then calling for a strategic British withdrawal from Northern Ireland. There was certainly substance to Haughey's assertion that because of Northern Ireland's troubles it could not be solved as a problem 'internal to the province'; it needed an 'Irish dimension', a position eventually accepted by Britain. Haughey's periodic engagement, or lack of it, with the border question was the result of a combination of 'ideological republicanism, ruthless pragmatism and political opportunism'. His grandstanding achieved little and he made no effort to understand unionism; nor was there any general acceptance of his idea of a 'unitary state'; his dislike of the border, however, was genuine.[4]

The hunger strikes of 1981, which saw ten die after the ultimate protest against withdrawal of 'special category' status from republican paramilitary prisoners, complicated matters and raised interesting questions about whether the emotional and political cross-border empathy that briefly existed during the early years of the Troubles could be reignited. As Thomas Hennessey points out, the hunger strikes were a bigger problem for the Dublin government than they were for the London government.[5] But once again London betrayed its ignorance of Irish history in how it exacerbated the situation. Haughey's successor, Garret FitzGerald, was later to aver that his main concern about Thatcher had been her lack of a sense of the importance of history, and biographical work on Thatcher reinforces the consequences of this disregard. As Richard English noted, 'Irish history could certainly have made clear the degree to which Irish nationalists might be mobilised to sympathise with republican prisoners, despite not having supported the violence that had caused such republicans to be put in prison in the first place.'[6]

But there was also caustic comment that sympathy south of the border was shallow and prisoners demanded that the southern government intervene, to no avail.[7] Well-known Irish folk singer Christy Moore was invited to visit the prisoners in the H Blocks (Maze prison) and asked to compose a song that would draw more southern Irish attention to the hunger strikes to counteract what Moore described as 'silence verging on total apathy'.[8] His response was 'Ninety Miles to Dublin Town', which included the verse

Though its ninety miles from Dublin it seems so far away
It's like we're getting more support from the USA
Now you've heard the story of this living hell
Remember ninety miles away I'm in my H-Block cell.[9]

It was a stinging rebuke, but protest songs were the least of the Irish government's worries; they also had to contend with the media attention the hunger strikes generated, internationally and nationally, though the emphasis in newspapers differed; the *Irish Independent* editorialised in March 1981 that those in the Republic were 'more preoccupied with other matters'.[10] Southern journalists also felt hamstrung, believing that if they were critical of the handling of Northern Ireland they would be depicted as IRA sympathisers.[11] Section 31 of the Broadcasting Act, imposed since 1971, was also relevant, prohibiting interviews with those perceived to be supportive of paramilitaries. For some, this was essential to prevent terrorists using the airwaves to promote and justify their aims, but for others it was regarded as an instrument of state censorship that simplified the conflict and compounded further ignorance. Section 31, it has been argued, was about 'amplifying one definition of a situation' in order to counteract 'a leaky national consensus', with those who questioned it accused of not being committed to the democratic state, but the result was 'zero public pressure on the Southern body politic to actively engage with what was happening north of the Border' along with 'insipid responses to injustices'.[12] These injustices were also manifest in the Republic as the human rights of those suspected of subversive activities or sympathies were frequently violated.[13] Overall, various censorship controls arguably left 'viewers in Ireland and Britain bereft of the means to understand the underlying causes of the conflict'.[14] Some of those in border areas and in the North did, however, have access to a greater range of media than in the South owing to the transmission of Ulster television and BBC Northern Ireland, which were unavailable to most in the Republic in the 1970s.

The election of hunger striker Bobby Sands as an MP in April 1981 (with 30,492 votes), the month before his death, was referred to by Chris Glennon of the *Irish Independent* as 'profoundly disappointing to all political parties in the Dáil'.[15] Haughey, it seemed, fell between two stools – not wanting to alienate either Irish republicans or the British government – and stayed quiet, but he also paid an electoral price when two anti H-Block candidates, Paddy Agnew and Kieran Doherty, were successful in the general election of 1981 (out of nine candidates who stood) and deprived him of a majority, meaning he could not form a government (leading republicans from both sides of the border had canvassed for the hunger strikers). But whatever about the emotionalism generated by the strikes and the enmity towards Thatcher, the southern media was consistent in editorialising that the IRA could not expect general support from the Republic if the violence continued.

In 1983–4, Taoiseach Garret FitzGerald convened the New Ireland Forum in Dublin, intended to achieve a consensus among constitutional nationalist parties. John Hume had pushed for its formation against the grain of historic hostility to the idea of an all-Ireland forum to discuss the future of Northern Ireland. It was partly, as he saw it, about preserving the SDLP's relevance in the face of a potential Sinn Féin challenge (that party emboldened by the hunger strikes and the resultant electoral dividend) by getting the Irish government to bring home to the British government the measure of its responsibility for the Northern Ireland crisis and forcing it to respond to concrete proposals. But it was also about attempting to formulate a more inclusive Irish 'identity', a word repeatedly used.[16] The forum's report committed national- ists to recognising the validity of both nationalist and unionist identities and for them to be protected 'in equally satisfactory, secure and durable, political, administrative and symbolic' form. Though the forum's preferred solution was a 'unitary state', it also underlined nationalists' openness to proposals other than a united Ireland, including a federal/co-federal or joint authority solution. But Thatcher made it clear in response that three constitutional options for Northern Ireland were 'out' – a unified Ireland, a con- federation system and joint authority.

Another thing ruled out in 1984 was the redrawing of the border; a secret plan was discussed by the UK cabinet to bring some predominantly Catholic areas into the Republic to 'produce a more homogeneous population in Northern Ireland' but it was ditched, with Northern Ireland secretary Jim Prior insisting it would be considered only 'if we were faced with imminent civil war or as a result of civil war but I do not believe we have reached that stage'.[17] Sir David Goodall, one of the diplomats negotiating with the Irish government, also recorded that late one night at Chequers Thatcher made the 'outrageous' proposal that if the northern Catholic population wanted to be in the South '"well why don't they move over there? After all, there was a big movement of population in Ireland, wasn't there?"' Goodall recalled, 'Nobody could think what it was. So finally I said, you are talking about Cromwell? She said, "That's right, Cromwell."'[18]

Once again, Thatcher was betraying her ignorance of Irish history; Cromwell had been responsible for a bloody, sectarian conquest of Ireland in the mid seventeenth century, a period during which up to 30 per cent of the population may have perished.[19] Sir Charles Powell, Thatcher's private secretary at this time, also suggested she wanted the Irish border to be redrawn: 'she thought that if we had a straight line border, not one with all those kinks and wiggles in it, it would be easier to defend', only to be told by Lord Armstrong, the cabinet secretary, of the folly of her thinking: 'it wasn't as simple as that because the nationalist communities were not all in one place'.[20] Nor was the idea of sealing the border, mentioned as a 'nuclear option' as early as 1973, remotely feasible:

> While stationed on the border, one officer jotted down what it would take to seal the whole length; 303 miles of mesh fencing; a vehicle track along the entire length; a hinterland security fence; 360,000 explosive charges; 165 miles of vehicle hazards, such as ditches and steel spikes, a hundred pillboxes, a hundred concrete observation towers. The defence would also need command posts, bunkers, dogs, dog runs and thousands of arc lights. All of that before the boots on the ground are considered.[21]

Thatcher made one brief visit to the border and viewed it

'from the window of a high-speed helicopter. She was gone in half an hour.'[22]

The efforts of John Hume and others in the US meant Thatcher was subsequently leaned on to relent in relation to the involvement of Irish governments in the affairs of Northern Ireland. Taoiseach Garret FitzGerald subsequently undertook negotiations with the British government leading to the 1985 Anglo-Irish Agreement and Haughey as leader of the opposition complained of an unacceptable and unconstitutional recognition of partition, even though the agreement built on some of his earlier initiatives and involved formal British recognition of an Irish role in Northern Ireland, to the disgust of unionists. The Anglo-Irish Agreement was described at the time as involving the British government inviting the Irish government 'to share in the burden of administering the troubled province of northern Ireland' and a 'dramatic shift in Prime Minister Thatcher's position ... never before has Britain acknowledged that Ireland has a legal role to play in governing the north'.

The agreement, it was asserted at the time, 'contradicts ... the belief that the North is exclusive British territory, that its affairs are purely an internal British concern'. With it, 'the two governments promised that the constitutional status of Northern Ireland could only be changed with the consent of the majority of the people there'. But the reaction to the agreement also underlined, in the words of deputy editor of the *Belfast Telegraph*, Barry White, 'Northern Ireland's Protestant unionists and Roman Catholic nationalists have never been further apart'.[23]

The Anglo-Irish Agreement's fourth article asserted it was the declared policy of Britain to encourage a devolved government in the North that would be acceptable to both sides of the community; Article 5 included the objectives of accommodating the rights and identities of the two communities, protecting human rights and preventing discrimination. As former US ambassador to Ireland William Shannon observed, 'unlike previous attempts to resolve communal antagonisms in the North through regional institutions that required unionist co-operation for their success, this agreement is entirely between the sovereign governments in London and Dublin'.[24] That, however, was also its weakness, and the consequences of insufficient engagement with representatives of Northern Ireland's two communities was recognised in the shift in positions that occurred in subsequent years.

Some of the political reminiscences about the 1980s underline the fractiousness and occasional wackiness of the thinking about the border in the context of fraught Anglo-Irish exchanges. Thatcher was no lover of Northern Ireland; after she and FitzGerald signed the Anglo-Irish Agreement and celebrated with a glass of champagne, FitzGerald raised the question of seeking support from the International Fund for Ireland, envisaged under the agreement to promote the social and economic development of areas in Ireland affected by the Troubles, which by the mid 1980s had resulted in the deaths of over 2,500 people.

'"More money for these people?" she said, waving her hand in the general direction of Northern Ireland. "Look at their schools; look at their roads. Why should they have more money? I need that money for my people in England who don't have anything like this."' FitzGerald recalled that he 'was frankly quite nonplussed at this singular declaration of English nationalism'.[25]

In 1986 FitzGerald and Thatcher were attempting to hold the line on the Anglo-Irish Agreement in the teeth of visceral unionist opposition and they met in December in London: Thatcher was blunt in how she assessed the border security situation: 'You,' she told him, 'haven't the resources to maintain protection on the other side of the border.' Thatcher wanted helicopters on the border with the right to fly five miles in either direction, or what she called 'a broad corridor around the border. That disappeared!' FitzGerald however, praised the RUC for working in conjunction with the Gardaí on the issue but concluded, bluntly and bleakly: 'both forces have a next-to-impossible Border to watch'. Thatcher responded, intriguingly, 'yes, we got it wrong in 1921'. Thatcher also wondered, as noted by Irish cabinet secretary Dermot Nally, if she could continue to send young soldiers 'to their death in Northern Ireland'[26] (the official Ministry of Defence figure of servicemen killed during the Troubles is 763). FitzGerald also asserted, 'so many people from the North come down to the South and live there. We have 200 people from the North in our jails. You can have them back any time you want!' Thatcher's response was, 'I don't want them. You can have all the Nationalists in the North if you like!'

Thatcher also complained in relation to the Anglo-Irish Agreement, 'You've got the glory and I've got the problems,' and she asked could he think of amending Articles 2 and 3 of the Irish constitution, but FitzGerald responded that nobody in the South had suggested the Anglo-Irish Agreement was 'a step towards a United Ireland'.[27] In her memoirs, Thatcher scorned the Anglo-Irish Agreement as having failed because it did not deliver on greater security co-operation; nor did it bring a reduction in violence; indeed 'it was the only major policy initiative of her premiership which she renounced'.[28]

The DUP was also determined to insist the Anglo-Irish Agreement had not improved border security. In trying to make that point, DUP deputy leader and MP Peter Robinson made a fool of himself and demonstrated his cowardice in August 1986 when he joined a loyalist mob for an 'invasion' of Clontibret, one of several border crossing points in North Monaghan in the Republic that were targeted to supposedly demonstrate that the Anglo-Irish Agreement had failed to produce better cross-border security and to, in their own words, 'seize the border'. It turned violent and menacing; some of the loyalists wore paramilitary uniforms, carried cudgels and iron bars, daubed slogans and attacked Gardaí, two of whom had to fire over their heads. Robinson was arrested and charged, scoring a spectacular own goal: he had been caught 'running away from the scene'. He faced initial charges of unlawful assembly, malicious damage and assault.[29] The case eventually came before the Special Criminal Court in Dublin, where he pleaded guilty and had to pay a fine of £17,500. The fine was in Irish pounds, or punts, not the sterling used in Northern Ireland, and he was subsequently labelled 'Peter the Punt' by certain wags. Justice Barr condemned the loyalists' 'grossly offensive, provocative, cowardly and terrifying attack'.[30]

British and Irish officials continued to exchange papers and thoughts throughout the 1980s. Michael Lillis, head of the Anglo-Irish division in the Irish Department of Foreign Affairs, and David Goodall on the British side were important players in relation to this; they had a discussion in Oxford in September 1983 and Lillis referred to the recent decision by the Irish electorate in a referendum to insert a pro-life amendment in the Irish constitution (giving equal right to the life of the mother and the unborn) to provide a double lock against abortion in the Republic (it was already legally prohibited), suggesting it would damage the Irish government's desire to remove Protestant and liberal concerns about the Republic's Catholic ethos. While this might be regrettable, Lillis suggested 'it would also have the merit of clarifying the situation and forcing nationalist opinion to face up to the reality of partition', and that unification 'was at best a long-term aspiration, not a political objective'.[31] But that was also contradictory, given the extent of fundamentalist Protestantism and stringent attitudes to abortion in Northern Ireland.

In 1987 Willie Whitelaw, the first secretary of state for Northern Ireland and close to Thatcher, had a private conversation with

Noel Dorr, the Irish ambassador in London, and he expressed the view that if power sharing in Northern Ireland could be success-fully achieved, 'the importance of the border would fade away over 50 years or so ... then unity would be a real possibility'.[32] But there was no sign of any thaw that would make that likely and debate about the validity of Northern Ireland and the border con-tinued. In 1989 Ulster-born economist Tom Wilson argued that Protestants had been more tolerant than their critics portrayed, but also that the ailing Republic did not have the wealth to replace British subvention of Northern Ireland and was still too much of a Catholic state for a Catholic people to embrace Protestants. He rejected the idea that majority determination should decide the status of the North; what was needed was fuller integration into the UK because Northern Ireland's instability was fuelled by too much uncertainty about its status.[33]

The following year, in *Unfinished Business*, southern histo-rian Liam de Paor insisted the Irish nation was coterminous with the island and stretched back 1,500 years but that the 'Perfidious Albion' approach to discussing the border was 'humbug'. The Irish question, he argued, had always been an Anglo-Irish ques-tion and the solution was an independent Northern Ireland guar-anteed by Britain and the Republic.[34] Political scientist John H. Whyte's analysis focused instead on an 'internal conflict' between Catholics and Protestants in his influential *Interpreting North-ern Ireland* the same year, envisaging decentralised solutions for different areas of Northern Ireland depending on their religious compositions.[35] In relation to attitudes in the North to reunifica-tion, Whyte identified twenty-five polls between 1973 and 1989, and there were broad consistencies. A united Ireland had minus-cule support from Protestants, far from complete support from Catholics, and the solution that attracted most support from both communities was power sharing.[36]

Whatever about the high politics that governed the border and the diplomacy and papers that analysed it, what did it mean in the 1980s to those living on or near it?

During his tour of the border region in 1986 for what became the 1987 book *Walking Along the Border*, journalist and novelist Colm Tóibín walked out of Derry and in half an hour was in the Republic, where the price of petrol, alcohol, cars and televisions was much higher: 'no one would dream of smuggling from the South to the North'.[37] A number of things were striking about his journey, including the meandering complexity of the border; to get to Castlederg in Tyrone, on the border with Donegal, for example, he was warned by one guider 'that I would go into the South, into the North, into the South again and back into the North. "How will I know whether I'm in the North or South?" I said to him. "You won't know" he replied, managing a gruff sort of smile.'[38]

The toll the violence of the previous twenty years had taken was also manifest, generating watchfulness, fearfulness and lack of trust; it had also destroyed businesses through intimidation and bombs, or the extension of checkpoints and military zones ('people in Strabane would see a thirty-two-vehicle convoy wade through the town in the middle of the night full of supplies for the new army checkpoint at Clady'). There was a constant feeling of the visitor in a divided society being 'unsure of my ground'.[39] But there were pockets of hope and cross-community co-operation also, including an artists' retreat in Annaghmakerrig in Monaghan that was supported by the arts councils of both North and South.

Tóibín also wrote with a wryness about the absurdity of a few minutes in either direction involving psychological readjustment: on a boat trip on Lough Erne, 'we weren't sure whether we were in the North or the South so after dinner we set out to investigate which state we were in'. As for having post-dinner drinks, with closing time in one pub, 'for further drinking it was necessary to return across the border'.[40] Margaret Thatcher had been correct about the border's 'kinks and wiggles', and they existed amidst strikingly beautiful, if desolate and confusing landscapes. Those traversing its terrain were often alone, like Tóibín and later Garrett Carr, as recounted in *The Rule of the Land: Walking Ireland's Border* (2017). As he trailed into the Cooley Mountains Carr noted, 'you need local knowledge or, like me, a detailed Ordnance Survey map to know which is the border. I find an apple tree growing straight out of the line. A coincidence, I wonder, that the tree took root in the border line, or did someone plant it there as a marker? There is no one to ask on these unpopulated slopes. I will not see a single person all morning.'[41]

The nature of living in a border area was also central to the work of Eugene McCabe with his house right on the divide; the driveway of his farm crossed from Monaghan into Fermanagh and back again. McCabe wrote of the border counties as 'a dim, hidden country, crooked scrub ditches of whin and thorns stunted in sour putty land; bare, spade-ribbed fields ... housing a stony-faced people living from rangy cattle and welfare handouts ... To them a hundred years was yesterday, two hundred the day before.'[42]

McCabe used the lonesome landscape to great effect in *Death and Nightingales* (1992), set in the 1880s in a claustrophobic, provincial world where there is much tension between Catholics and Protestants in the terrain that was to become the border landscape. The tense household of Beth Winters encapsulates the religious divide in Fermanagh but also the interdependencies; the Protestant Billy has a successful limestone quarry which is heavily dependent on business with the Catholic archdiocese, but it is also a suspicious, class-riven world; as Fr Leo McManus muses, 'hungry views and sour land can make the best people in the world sullen and dangerous.'[43]

6

No Victory for Either Tradition

A century on from the setting of Eugene McCabe's fiction, violence continued to scar the border area and other parts of Northern Ireland; exceptional revulsion was generated by an IRA bomb that killed eleven people in November 1987 in Enniskillen during the annual wreath-laying at the war memorial. The following year, John Hume controversially decided to engage in direct dialogue with Sinn Féin president Gerry Adams, and thus the IRA, to seek an end to the violence. Hume's insistence was that fixation with the border should not obscure the need for humanity:

> Ireland is not a romantic dream; it is not a flag; it is 4.5 million people divided into two powerful traditions. The solution will be found not on the basis of victory for either, but on the basis of agreement and a partnership between both. The real division of Ireland is not a line drawn on the map but in the minds and hearts of its people.[1]

There were also shifts in thinking on the British side. Secretary of State for Northern Ireland Peter Brooke's Whitbread Speech of November 1990 was particularly significant: 'The British government has no selfish or strategic or economic interest in Northern Ireland: our role is to help, enable and encourage. Britain's purpose ... is not to occupy, oppress or exploit but to ensure democratic debate and free democratic choice.' A year earlier he had stated the British government would be 'flexible and imaginative' if the IRA's campaign ceased, stressing that there would then be a 'totally new situation'.[2]

In succeeding Margaret Thatcher as prime minister in 1990 John Major, according to Lord Robin Butler, who served as cabinet secretary under both, 'didn't have emotionally in his political background that link with the unionists ... the Conservatives were no longer the Conservative and Unionist Party'. Major, by his own admission 'knew very little of Northern Ireland'.[3] This was indicative of an enduring theme: British interest in Northern Ireland was never as deep as Northern Ireland politicians would have liked. William Shannon remarked acidly in 1986, regarding a 1984 session in the House of Commons on the New Ireland Forum, 'as usual most members of Parliament chose a debate on Northern Ireland as the time to go answer their mail or have a drink with a constituent'.[4] But such lack of emotional engagement could also be a positive when it came to the business of negotiating a solution, and Major's lack of baggage was an advantage.

The words of Peter Brooke at Whitbread also found their way into the Downing Street Declaration of 1993 in which the British government formally disavowed any 'selfish, strategic or economic interest in Northern Ireland' and promised to act as facilitators for an agreement that might 'embrace the totality of relationships'. Fianna Fáil Taoiseach Albert Reynolds also indicated that contentious aspects of the Irish constitution might be altered as part of a broader settlement.[5] In the words of conflict studies expert Eamonn O'Kane, 'The transformation in the situation by 1993 was remarkable with not only the unionists being more receptive to the intergovernmental overtures but the two governments being more aware of the need to make these overtures if their wider objectives were to be fulfilled.'[6]

An IRA ceasefire followed, as did talk of a new era and the importance of dialogue that eventually led to all-party talks, with David Trimble trying to carry a reluctant and divided Ulster Unionist Party, that culminated in the Belfast Agreement of 1998, frequently referred to as the Good Friday Agreement. It included a guarantee of the union of Northern Ireland with Britain and the principle of consent was then enshrined in the constitution of the Republic (a united Ireland could only be brought about 'with the consent of a majority of the people, democratically expressed, in both jurisdictions in the island'). But crucially, with this agreement, the 'principle of popular sovereignty is replacing the principle of monarchical sovereignty as the legitimating doctrine of Northern Ireland'.[7] The agreement stated it 'would be wrong to make any change in the status of Northern Ireland save with the consent of a majority of its people', and that recognition would be given to the right 'of all the people of Northern Ireland to identify themselves and be accepted as Irish or British, or both, as they may so choose, and accordingly confirm that their right to hold both British and Irish citizenship is accepted by both governments and would not be affected by any future change in the status of Northern Ireland'.

Though it was rejected by the DUP, the more civic-minded members of the Ulster Unionist Party could claim it was necessary to compromise to allow a fresh start for Northern Ireland and that it had secured the Union, the principle of consent and the eradication of the Republic's territorial claim. The republicans obtained a share of power in Northern Ireland, cross-border bodies, the disbandment of the RUC, acceptance that they had fought a war and prisoners could be released and the possibility of a border poll if it appeared likely to the Northern Ireland secretary 'that a majority of those voting would express a wish that Northern Ireland should ... form part of a united Ireland'. What all this amounted to was recognition of the need for accommodation of change and self-determination. Britain adapted its assertion of sovereignty over Northern Ireland contained in the 1920 Government of Ireland Act, with the future of the province left to its inhabitants: 'Thus the consent principle permitted both governments to disengage themselves from embarrassing inherited position.'[8] Part of the force of the Belfast Agreement lay in the idea, articulated by John Hume, that a poll conducted in both parts of Ireland simultaneously 'would carry a moral authority which would be very difficult for those locked into the theology of the past to ignore'.[9] The result of the referendum vote in Northern Ireland was Yes: 71.12 per cent, No, 28.88 per cent; in the Republic Yes: 94.39 per cent and No: 5.61 per cent.[10]

The vote was understandably tinged with caution given the history of Northern Ireland, but there was no disputing, in the words of political scientist Tom Garvin, that 'the constitutional relationships between Britain and Ireland and between the two parts of Ireland have changed profoundly'. The opportunity that was missed in 1921 and subsequently due to a passionate refusal to 'accept politics as a means of engineering peace among peoples with apparently irreconcilable aspirations and purposes' was confronted, breaking the province out of the 'historical and structural trap' of 1920–23.[11]

There was no shortage of declarations of change, history making, new eras and transformations in April and May 1998 as a result of the referendums. Historian Roy Foster wrote optimistically of new definitions of Irishness and observed that the details of the agreement 'reflect the most significant statement of popular opinion since 1921 on the basic question of Irish political identity [and] history, and not only Irish history shows all the time what disasters occur when the borders of states, nations and geography are drawn to fit some preconceived theory'.[12] Alvin Jackson, specialist in the history of Ulster unionism, suggested with the signing of the agreement, the Unionist signatories 'had now formally abandoned a crude majoritarianism and had accepted the reality of cross-border institutions', while the British had recognised that 'it is for the people of Ireland alone' to decide on the issue of unification.[13]

The agreement also acknowledged, as had the Anglo-Irish Agreement before it, that a majority in Northern Ireland wanted maintenance of the Union; more than this, the deal explicitly underlined for the first time the legitimacy of this unionist position. Paul Bew characterised the vote as achieving for the agreement 'a local legitimacy always denied to Sunningdale'.[14] Given the acceptance by the Irish government that the entitlement to British citizenship of those born in Northern Ireland would remain in the event of reunification, 'Irish citizenship is perhaps now best seen as transcending the border rather than subverting it'.[15]

The chorus of hopefulness was cruelly shattered, however, on 15 August 1998, when a car bomb was detonated in Omagh town in Tyrone while the streets were packed with shoppers, killing twenty-nine people, including a woman heavily pregnant with twins. Beyond devastating, it was the biggest single atrocity in the history of the Troubles and the work of dissident republicans, styled the 'Real IRA', some of whom were based in the Republic. The bomb had been transported over the border and the victims came from both sides of it as well as England and Spain. Despite an extensive cross-border police investigation in its aftermath, no one was criminally convicted of a crime that prompted the poet

John Montague to despair that 'History creaks on its bloody hinge and the unspeakable is done again.'[16]

British Prime Minister Tony Blair had provided a soundbite on the eve of the Belfast Agreement, stating that he could feel 'the hand of history' on his shoulder in relation to a breakthrough. But putting the historic agreement into practice – and it was vehemently opposed by the DUP – was to be a tortuous process, and in private it was the hand of history around his neck that most irked Blair as the siege mentality of diehard unionists and the ambiguous assertions of republicans delayed progress. After a meeting with representatives of the Orange Order in June 1999 there was a brief discussion about Ireland at the Labour Party's parliamentary meeting and Blair did not attempt to hide his exasperation: he found the Orange brethren 'unbelievable people ... there is nothing more irritating than sitting in a room with someone who claims to be British but who treats you as though you are nothing to do with Britain, even though you are the prime minister'.[17] That went to the heart of the unionist mentality that the original creation of Northern Ireland had facilitated, and despite the 1998 agreement, many unionists still felt the need to look inwards, believing neither London nor Dublin nor, of course, Northern Ireland nationalists could be trusted.

This was matched by an often-duplicitous republicanism, capable of sending different and contradictory messages about whether this was a final settlement or a bridge to advance the quest for a united Ireland, which was perhaps why Blair felt they needed to be 'brought to the precipice and asked to look over it'.[18] This is why so much of the politics of Northern Ireland was still for some a 'zero-sum' quarrel. But there was also the added complication of the standing of Ulster unionism, given the waning of Britain's international status. The identity of Ulster loyalism had for so long been interwoven with British empire that the decline of 'Britishness' inevitably made the Protestants of Ulster feel cast adrift – or, as Tom Bartlett put it in 1998: 'If Ulster is British what is British?' Was unionism as a political creed, given the momentum behind devolution in Scotland and Wales, and especially growing Scottish nationalism, on a road to nowhere?[19] Or on a road across the border to a united Ireland?

Sworn foes were eventually able to share power in Northern Ireland with an executive and assembly, though for every step forward there was constant dragging back; a frosty tolerance, easily unhinged. Along the way there were postponed assembly elections and numerous claims that the Belfast Agreement was 'dead', the firm IRA statement of July 2005 ('All volunteers have been instructed to assist the development of purely political and democratic programmes through exclusively peaceful means'), followed by verifiable arms decommissioning and numerous twists and turns before the 2006 St Andrews Agreement committed the DUP to sharing power with republicans and Sinn Féin to supporting the police, with a power-sharing government to follow in 2007. It seemed in 1998 that the Belfast Agreement had vindicated the moderates – the SDLP and the Ulster Unionists – but in the long run the so-called 'extremes' of the DUP and Sinn Féin were the winners. There was an element of history repeating itself in this regard, as a similar transformation happened in the South in the period 1922–32, when the anti-treaty republicans lost the vote over the Anglo-Irish Treaty and were crushed in the civil war, only to win power less than ten years later.

Ultimately, the most obvious thaws were in Anglo-Irish and North–South relations; those sharing power in Northern Ireland were less effusive about what held them together and their capacity to overcome what still divided them, but crucially, there was no return to the depths of violence that had endured for almost thirty years at the cost of 3,700 lives. There was also the spectre of DUP leader Ian Paisley, as first minister for Northern Ireland, emphasising during an outbreak of foot-and-mouth disease among English cattle the 'clear blue sea' between Britain and Northern Ireland, choosing to stress Northern Ireland's shared interest with the Republic rather than Britain in facing this threat.[20]

The physical border remained, but it became much less contentious and the infrastructure and security apparatus around it began to be dismantled. In April 1999 a statue was unveiled to mark the reopening of one border crossing point between Northern Ireland and the Republic: the Aghalane bridge, near the town of Belturbet in Cavan, reconnecting the townlands of Aghalane in Fermanagh and Lagan in Cavan. It replaced a bridge that had been blown up in 1972 by loyalist paramilitaries. With the reopening, the main route between Dublin, Fermanagh and Donegal, and the local route between the towns, villages and townlands that were formerly linked by 'longstanding and close social, family, farming and commercial connections that crossed the border', were freed. This widely reported reopening 'was strongly framed by its practical purpose in regenerating a border area that suffered' when the local economic cross-border links had been severed. It was also 'a symbolic moment and made to stand for wider possibilities for reconnection and reconciliation'.[21]

The Belfast Agreement also alluded to the relevance of joint UK and Irish membership of the EU and with the peace process, EU money was poured into reconciliation ventures in Northern Ireland. In 2000 the EU Commission established a special Northern Ireland task force 'to examine how Northern Ireland could benefit more from EU policies', the first time the commission had, in its own words, created 'a close partnership specifically with one region' in this way. What also made the EU dimension significant was the importance of open borders to the overall EU project and the perception of the EU as being 'neutral' regarding Northern

Ireland in a way the UK and Irish governments could not always manage.[22] In 2010, EU Commission chief José Manuel Barroso noted EU institutions had contributed more than £2.5 billion to Northern Ireland since 1990, while Northern Ireland's first minister, the DUP's Peter Robinson, who succeeded Paisley in 2008, said Northern Ireland would have been a 'very much worse place ... if it hadn't been for the significant funds that have come from Europe'.[23]

Europe was also the platform from which a 'shared history' for the different communities in Ireland could be remembered and commemorated, one of the most obvious examples being the Irish nationalists and unionists who fought with the British army at the Slaughter of the Somme in 1916. Such attention to inclusive commemoration, alongside the peace process and the sense of an 'invisible' or 'soft' Irish border, greatly improved relations between North and South; ultimately, up to 30,000 were travelling over the border each day, and that was convenient and valuable for both jurisdictions. The peace process also resulted in the establishment of InterTrade Ireland, to promote North–South business development, Waterways Ireland to manage the island's inland waterways, Safefood, a health awareness agency, and Tourism Ireland, to market the island as a unit.[24]

In the years after the Belfast Agreement, North–South co-operation became, in the words of Andy Pollak, first director of the Centre for Cross Border Studies established in 1999, 'a quiet cross-border success story', prompting Peter Robinson to assert in 2009, 'I don't think the relationship between Northern Ireland and the Irish republic has ever been better than it is at the present time.' The cross-border centre combined a strong research focus on the social and economic dimensions of border areas with practical support for cross-border co-operation. Numerous specialist research centres were paralleled by the efforts of local community activists and by cultural engagements with borderland histories, experiences and identities.[25]

The Republic became increasingly secularised and socially liberal in the late twentieth and early twenty-first century (divorce legalised, male homosexual acts legalised, same-sex marriage approved in a referendum, the repeal of a constitutional amendment preventing the legalisation of abortion) in parallel with the collapse of authority of a much discredited and shamed Catholic Church. This meant one of the original and potent arguments of Ulster Protestants against Irish unity – that it would amount to Rome rule and Protestants would be victimised – no longer carried much credence; indeed, Northern Ireland looked increasingly socially conservative in contrast to the Republic. This had been apparent for decades; in the late 1970s, for example, the DUP's 'Save Ulster from Sodomy' campaign was a reaction to the bravery of Jeff Dudgeon of the Northern Ireland Gay Rights Association, who took the British government to the European Court of Human Rights on the basis that the failure to apply to Northern Ireland the 1967 legislation legalising homosexuality in England and Wales discriminated against Northern Ireland gay people's right to privacy. He eventually won his case, but the first Belfast Gay Pride festival was not organised until 1991, at a time when a Protestant minister referred to the gay community as 'worse than dogs'. Such rhetoric was commonplace in the North for many years.[26] Nor was marriage equality extended to Northern Ireland.

Southern Ireland did not, however, fully embrace the notion of an all-island political vision. In 2011 Sinn Féin's Martin McGuinness, a former IRA leader, took time out from his role as deputy first minister of Northern Ireland to contest the Irish presidency. McGuinness showed annoyance at various stages in a campaign that resulted in him receiving 13.7 per cent of the vote, a solid but not especially impressive total, and certainly less than

Sinn Féin, the only Irish political party with a sizeable presence on both sides of the border, had hoped and expected. One thing that irked McGuinness was the reality of the partitionist mindset in the Republic, and during the campaign he specifically referred to the gulf between North and South, a remonstrance from northern republicans that was decades old.

McGuinness complained that he was treated differently from the other candidates, which was true. The *Belfast Telegraph* retorted that none of the other candidates 'stands accused of heading a murderous organisation', but, as observed by journalist Gail Walker, such treatment did leave 'one small niggling conundrum; if he's not presidential material down there, why is he deputy first minister up here?'[27] Mary Lou McDonald, who took over the presidency of Sinn Féin from Gerry Adams in 2018, was subsequently to characterise the treatment of McGuinness during the election as 'utterly repulsive', for which she blamed the 'southern establishment', a reaction to one of Ireland's best-known current-affairs anchors, Miriam O'Callaghan, asking McGuinness during the campaign, 'How do you square ... with your God the fact that you were involved in the murder of so many people?'[28] McDonald translated this as 'who are you from Derry to presume that you are Irish enough or that your citizenship is of sufficient standing that you should contest for the position of First Citizen? ... It was a partitionist mentality.' She also maintained it was about class: 'the hungry streets of Derry meeting the comfortable affluence of Dublin 4' (a postcode associated with the wealthy Irish establishment).[29]

This, however, was a conveniently selective interpretation. Mary McAleese, a native of County Down, after a vitriolic election campaign in which she was somewhat under siege for being what one journalist called an 'upwardly mobile Northern Gael' and whose own journalistic career had been stymied in the South partly as a result of her perceived Ulster nationalist sympathies, had been comfortably elected president of Ireland in 1997 on a 'bridge-building' theme, promising to reconcile unionism and nationalism. Despite murmurs from her critics, she was not seen as tarnished by the excesses of the Troubles; indeed, her family had been a victim of sectarianism, and there may have been an element of the salving of guilty southern consciences in relation to historic attitudes to northern nationalists.

One of the most arresting moments of the 2011 campaign was when McGuinness was confronted in Athlone, Westmeath (in the middle of Ireland, not Dublin 4) by the son of army private Patrick Kelly, shot dead in 1983 during the rescue of businessman Don Tidey, who had been kidnapped by the IRA: he told McGuinness: 'I want justice for my father. I believe you know the names of the killers of my father and I want you to tell me who they are. You were on the Army Council of the IRA.'[30] This legacy had also followed Gerry Adams when he moved from northern to southern politics; he was elected a TD in 2011 but remained a polarising politician on both sides of the border, receiving much credit for persuading most of the republican movement to embrace the peace process while continually facing questions about republican violence during the Troubles and his own incredible denials of his previous IRA membership.

But much heat was also taken out of the border question, and even humour about it could breathe. For two weeks in September 2000 it had its own pop-up interpretative centre; comedian Kevin McAleer joked that it was 'the best little border in the world', given its great endurance, far outlasting the border between east and west Germany. John Byrne, the instigator of the interpretative centre, compared the border to sex: something that people 'were reluctant to talk about'. One Monaghan farmer said that he felt fortunate that his father explained the facts of the border to him because many of his contemporaries were left to find out for themselves and as adults were embarrassed to discuss it with their children.[31]

Inventive artists were also absorbed by the border, including photographer Kate Nolan, whose fascination with frontiers brought her to the village of Pettigo, straddling the Donegal–Fermanagh border, for her project *Reframing the Border*. Rather than seeing the border people as in limbo she preferred the idea of them as an identity unto themselves, a 'third space in which physical borders create new ways of seeing and scheming, including the man who owned a bridge across the border; he bought a chip van on eBay and then put the van on it', so avoiding taxes as it was neither in the North nor the South.[32] Nolan was also interested in the perspective of children who had never seen a militarised Irish border and 'don't recognise a border – even a ritual as simple as going to get the dinner in the chipper could involve walking across the border' – and the ease of visiting a grandparent who lived five minutes over the border.[33]

This idea of a specific border people or identity also struck Garrett Carr when on his border travels in 2016: 'border people ... seemed to be giving name to an identity, a culture even.'[34] There was even, with the European soccer championships in France in June 2016, in which both Northern Ireland and Republic of Ireland teams participated, a cathartic sense of peaceful and supportive co-existence between northern and southern fans, summed up in the comment of the French sports newspaper *L'Equipe* on 22 June, 'for atmosphere, Ireland is unified'.[35]

And then, a day later, came the Brexit vote.

7

Brexit, Backstops and Brinkmanship

While 55.8 per cent of the Northern Ireland electorate who voted in the Brexit referendum opted to remain in the EU (although the DUP, unlike most northern politicians, supported Brexit), the overall UK vote meant, it seemed, that Northern Ireland would be exiting the EU against its will. Tricky questions came tumbling fast: was it the case that with Northern Ireland outside the EU, those northerners who wished to remain European citizens would be required to claim Irish citizenship, even if they saw themselves as British? The Belfast Agreement had included assertions about not changing the status of Northern Ireland without its people's consent and their right to be Irish or British citizens or both. While the issue of choice about status was framed in relation to the options of remaining part of the UK or Irish unification, the Brexit vote nonetheless raised legitimate, related concerns about self-determination and allegiance.

On initial reading, Brexit appeared to be a development that would harden the Irish border. But there was an alternative reading: given the tension and disunity in the UK, the desire of most in Northern Ireland to remain in the EU and the potential for Brexit to result in crippling trade barriers between North and South, it might make the case for Irish unity stronger. Would younger unionists who wanted to stay in the EU feel less trenchant than their parents' generation about their unionism? Would the desire of some of them to possess Irish passports reflect something more than opportunism? The number of applications for Irish passports in the first four months of 2018 increased by 25 per cent compared with the same period in 2016.[1]

EU subsidies provided through the Common Agricultural Policy at that stage represented 87 per cent of income for Northern Ireland farmers compared with 53 per cent for the UK overall. The importance of the border issue in economic terms was underlined by the fact that Northern Ireland exported £2.7 billion of goods to Ireland in 2015, representing 36 per cent of its total goods exports, and in some sectors, including energy and agriculture, 'it was feasible to talk of an all-island market ... and an all-island economy'.[2] There was also the enduring relevance of the comment by British economic affairs minister Peter Shore in 1967: 'When London gets a chill, Northern Ireland gets the 'flu and Derry gets pneumonia; it's that sort of relationship.'[3]

The tensions between North and South and London and Dublin grew manifest after the Brexit vote. Increasing ill-temper and no shortage of farce inevitably put a strain on Anglo-Irish relations, which, in the few years previously, especially with the successful state visit of Queen Elizabeth II to Ireland in 2011, and a return visit by Irish president Michael D. Higgins, had been regarded as at an all-time high. In the aftermath of the referendum, however, the Irish government had to go back to the business of emphasising both Irish distinctiveness from Britain and at the same time their common needs, a significant foreign policy challenge.

In July 2017 the new Taoiseach, Fine Gael's Leo Varadkar, not unreasonably pointed out that the Irish government was not going to 'design a border for the Brexiteers, because they're the ones who want a border', and it was hinted that an Irish government might assert a preference for a soft sea border between Ireland and Britain rather than a hard land border. The DUP angrily rejected the idea of a sea border, which was also later dismissed by the British government; were the Irish Sea to become, in effect, the border, those arriving from Britain to Belfast would face immigration and customs checks, as would those going in the other direction, which would involve Northern Ireland keeping the same customs regime as Ireland (staying in the customs union), and becoming economically separated from the rest of the UK.

But what the Irish government were confident of was that '[Ireland's] interests and the EU's interests were now indivisible'.[4] They were also content, it seemed, that there was more appreciation by the EU of the importance of the border as an issue of societal and political stability connected to the Belfast Agreement than just a technical, trade-related issue. Little appreciation of this had been shown in Britain; novelist Colm Tóibín, who had written of his travels around the border in the late 1980s, in an interview after the Brexit vote noted: 'No one in the world would claim it was a campaign run with Northern Ireland in mind. It's another example, in case we need one, of how little Northern Ireland matters to anyone in Britain.'[5]

Northern Ireland's first minister, the DUP's Arlene Foster, was mute about the notion of Northern Ireland having a 'special status' in the context of Brexit, and contemptuously dismissed the idea that Brexit could damage the peace process as 'outrageous commentary'. It was nothing of the sort. Historian Ian McBride noted that the Belfast Agreement

> clearly envisaged that Northern Ireland's future constitu-
> tional arrangements would be worked out in the context of

continuing partnership between the North and the South, and between politicians in London and Dublin. To remove Northern Ireland from Europe without its consent is not only morally wrong and politically risky; it is also a rejection of the fundamental bilateralism of the peace process.[6]

Senator George Mitchell, who chaired the Good Friday Agreement negotiations, when asked if Brexit was a breach of the Agreement, said 'the agreement plainly provides that the political status of Northern Ireland can be determined or changed only through a vote – and it's the informed consent through a vote – of the people of Northern Ireland'.[7]

Irish High Court judge Richard Humphreys argued that the terms of the agreement would still apply after Brexit, or even in the event of Irish unity ('Stormont would continue to legislate for the day-to-day affairs of Northern Ireland'); Article 3.1 of the Irish constitution deems unity to be the 'firm will' of the Irish people if consent has also been obtained in Northern Ireland, and it was suggested a simple majority of a poll in Northern Ireland would be enough to bring this about. But the 'British identity' of unionists would still have to be catered for, and Humphreys suggested reactivating Irish Commonwealth membership (which ceased in 1949), as it would 'open up new vistas for co-operation with the UK and other countries with which we have a common legal history'.[8]

Abandonment of recognition of partnership mixed with self-determination about status and citizenship in Northern Ireland – so painstakingly achieved over decades – had potentially very serious implications. The confidence and supply agreement between the DUP and the Conservative Party after the 2017 general election to keep the Tories in office called into obvious question the extent to which the UK government could be an

'honest broker' in Northern Ireland; at the same time, it continued to acknowledge the EU's 'unwavering support for the peace
process'. There was not only the irony of an embattled Theresa
May depending on stalwart (many would say extremist) defend-
ers of the Union in the DUP while attempting to keep on board
arch nationalists in her own party, but also the danger that Ireland
could once again become a pawn in relation to British political
priorities.

May was on record as insisting her party 'will never be neutral
in expressing support' for Northern Ireland to remain part of the
UK, an unwise declaration given the logic of the peace process.
The Irish government was wary, despite declarations of solidarity
from the rest of the EU, for the same simple reason Ireland always
had to be wary about the Tories and Ireland: 'solutions devised
in London are devised with English objectives in view ... where
we do not go is to London for solutions to the Ulster question'.[9]
May had remarked before the Brexit vote that it was 'inconceivable' that the invisible border in Ireland would not be affected by
Brexit and predicted 'border controls' if the referendum was carried. But her post-referendum talk was of a 'frictionless' border.[10]

In December 2017 there was an 'agreement' between the EU
and UK on moving to stage two of negotiations and promises of
a 'backstop' option for Northern Ireland, which would require
the UK to participate in a 'common regulatory area' with the
EU (in the event of no Brexit deal) to 'support North–South co-
operation, the all-island economy and the protection of the 1998
agreement'. There were assertions on the Irish side about 'cast-iron
guarantees' in relation to the Irish border as a result of this and the
extent to which the agreement was 'bullet-proof'. This was hot
air; the agreement was political, not legal; a ruse by the British
government to move to the next stage of the negotiations. Leo
Varadkar nonetheless made much political capital out of it and

threw in for good measure afterwards a commitment that never again would northern nationalists be 'abandoned' by an Irish government, a rare official acceptance that this is what had happened almost a century previously.

Brexit secretary David Davis referred to the agreement as a 'statement of intent' before he was forced to backtrack. The history of Anglo-Irish relations is a reminder of how agreements and phrases can be read in different ways, and there was much in the December 2017 EU–UK report that fell into that category along with, on the report's cover, 'the caveat that nothing is agreed until everything is agreed'. The protocol also referred specifically to continued North–South co-operation in environment, health, agriculture, transport, education and tourism, energy, telecommunications, broadcasting, inland fisheries, higher education and sport as well as safeguarding the common travel area and detailing protective measures around discrimination, equality and identity.

The way one historian of the border, Peter Leary, saw it in March 2018, there were 'broadly, three ways to avoid the return of customs checks and stations to the long-troubled Irish border': a united Ireland, a special arrangement for Northern Ireland, or a settlement covering the whole United Kingdom

> involving something similar to the existing customs union and probably some sort of commitment to regulatory alignment. None of these options are open to Theresa May ... A prisoner of her party, the DUP and her own hubris, for May to stay in office she has to reimpose a hard border ... The Irish, and Anglo-Irish, implications of this slow-motion car crash are increasingly well rehearsed.[11]

Talk of the 'constitutional integrity' of the UK as an excuse to reject a 'special status' for Northern Ireland post-Brexit was also too loose and uninformed and ignored the changes of the previous twenty years. The Belfast Agreement of 1998 had referred to 'changes' in British legislation and the constitution of Ireland 'relating to the constitutional status of Northern Ireland'. In passing the Northern Ireland Act of 1998, the British Parliament repealed the Government of Ireland Act of 1920, with the new Act to have effect 'notwithstanding any other previous enactment', while, as seen earlier, the Irish constitution was amended to declare 'a united Ireland shall only be brought about by peaceful means' and with the consent of a majority of both parts of Ireland. What it meant was that Northern Ireland had a different constitutional status from the rest of the UK.

There was also the endurance of doubts – which had always existed – about Britain's commitment to or interest in Northern Ireland, as well as an Irish government that was more vocal about Brexit as something that might ultimately require a revisiting of the issue of Irish unity but that was also cautious about the idea of a border poll. In December 2017 the polling company Lucid Talk found that, in the face of a 'hard' Brexit, 48 per cent of Northern Ireland's voters would opt for a united Ireland while 45 per cent would prefer to stay with an exited UK.[12] Before Brexit there had been numerous Northern Ireland Life and Times (NILT) surveys indicating falling expectations of a united Ireland and an increase in the number of Catholics who favoured staying in the UK. But it was difficult to see the plethora of opinion polls that began to appear on attitudes to unity as reliable; even after the referendum the pro-unity figure from NILT stood at 22 per cent, 'implying half the North's nationalist voters are not nationalist'.[13] This seemed unbelievably low, but other polls based on online panels and telephone interviews produced implausibly high pro-unity figures. Just how representative were they? How politicised had polling become?

Various polls in 2017 and 2018 suggested attitudes to unity had changed, but there were too many vagaries. In June 2018 an online survey conducted by Lucid Talk for the BBC found that 45 per cent of people in Northern Ireland wanted to remain as part of the UK, while 42.1 per cent said they would like to join the Republic of Ireland; 12.7 per cent said they didn't know. A significant finding was that fewer people in Northern Ireland thought of themselves as British than in any other UK region, at just 46.7 per cent compared to 58.6 per cent who called themselves Irish.[14] But another poll, by Ipsos MORI, found that just 21.1 per cent of people in Northern Ireland would vote for Irish unity after the UK left the EU. The poll, commissioned by academics at Queen's University Belfast, found that not even half of Catholics would vote for a united Ireland, with just 42.6 per cent favouring that option – although a large percentage, 26 per cent, were undecided.[15]

There were thus no guarantees that a united Ireland would be approved in any poll; while Sinn Féin had been quick to call for one after Brexit, under the terms of the Belfast agreement, by the summer of 2018 Sinn Féin was suggesting a poll on Irish unity should not be held while there was uncertainty around Brexit because it would not be conducive to 'maximising consent'. Sinn Féin President Mary Lou McDonald then backtracked on this, insisting a border poll would be imperative if Britain left the EU with no Brexit deal, while also insisting unionists who ignored the issue were putting their heads in the sand. It was the Irish government's stance that a border poll at that stage would not be at all 'helpful'.[16]

Nonetheless, the DUP's former leader Peter Robinson made a significant intervention in July 2018 by asserting in relation to a United Ireland, 'I don't expect my own house to burn down but I still insure it because it could happen.' Some viewed this as a demographic 'wake-up' call to unionists because the 2011 census showed that 48 per cent of Northern Ireland's population of 1.8 million came from Protestant homes while 45 per cent came from Catholic homes, but there were far more younger Catholics in education; this appeared to be a demographic curve heading towards a Catholic majority. Robinson's critics saw his mediation as an invitation to republican arsonists intent on politically burning their way to a united Ireland; he was even accused of becoming a 'Sinn Féin echo chamber'. Historian Peter Shirlow, from a unionist background, was less severe in his reaction; it was not just a recognition of demographic reality but also a pitch for Catholic middle-class support for Northern Ireland staying in the UK which Robinson had addressed previously; what he was essentially saying was, 'a traditional type of Unionism will not save the union'.[17]

As to the economic costs of unity, it was frequently highlighted that the British exchequer's subvention to Northern Ireland was in the region of €11 billion annually and its underdeveloped economy had an exceptional reliance on the public purse. It was estimated that the transfer from the UK exchequer accounted for between 20 and 25 per cent of Northern Ireland's GDP, and while there was some success in technology, food and pharmaceutical sectors, the peace process did not bring the economic investment and dynamism hoped for in Northern Ireland, the situation not helped by its dysfunctional politics. While the long-term potential for an expanded united Irish economy may have held out reasons for optimism, how the Republic would manage to absorb the cost of unification and replacing the UK subvention in the short term was a troubling question with predictions that it could reduce the Republic's living standards and national income by up to 15 per cent.[18]

What also remained problematic amidst any talk of unity was dealing with the reality of an Ulster unionism that may have been much weakened – power sharing collapsed in Northern Ireland in January 2017 and the consequent Northern Ireland assembly elections indicated that, for the first time, unionist parties no longer had an outright majority and 70 per cent of voters backed parties opposed to Brexit – but could not be ignored or coerced, and the need for the British government to court a DUP that was now propping up a Conservative party at war.

The aftermath of the Brexit referendum brought numerous reminders of the extent to which the policing and security infrastructure around the border had been largely dismantled as a result of the peace process and that there were many aspects of cross-border movement and co-operation quietly convenient and successful. These included cross-border social welfare and pension entitlements because the Common Travel Area between Britain and Ireland (founded upon administrative agreements in 1922 and 1952) provided for reciprocal rights between both countries, ensuring that British and Irish citizens could continue to travel freely between North and South and Britain and Ireland with the right to live, work, study and access welfare and other services in each other's countries. At the time of Brexit, 135,070 people in Ireland were in receipt of a UK pension and 34,238 people resident in the UK were in receipt of an Irish pension.[19]

Backed by European funding, a 'highly developed sphere of cross-border healthcare activity in Ireland' had also been advanced, reflected in Co-operation and Working Together (CAWT), an organisation whose 'mission is to improve the health and well being of the border populations, by working across boundaries and jurisdictions'.[20] Heart attacks in Donegal that could prove fatal if a long journey had to be made in the South to a specialist hospital, for example, could be treated successfully by a facility in nearby Derry: 'In one early project, a team from the University of Ulster found that along the border, 70,000 people could get quicker access to a GP out of hours by crossing the border (from either side) than they could in their own jurisdiction.'[21]

And, as Patrick Smyth of the *Irish Times* pointed out, the border was a sideshow if you were a European eel, a species endangered by overfishing and loss of habitat, their survival depending partly on whether the border between North and South could remain 'frictionless' on the Erne river at Ballyshannon. The protection of the eel was 'just one of 142 areas of North–South co-operation that are underpinned by joint obligations to EU regulations and the Belfast Agreement.'[22]

But the headline-grabbing border issues after Brexit were the high politics and political poker games between Britain and the EU. The European Council identified the 'unique circumstances on the island of Ireland' as one of the main issues to be dealt with in Brexit negotiations. Unionists also wanted to have their Brexit cake and to eat it across the border, essentially calling for the status quo in relation to freedom of movement of people, goods and services to be maintained.[23] Nigel Dodds insisted the DUP wanted a 'seamless border' but also wanted, in facing Brexit, to be no different 'from other parts of the UK'. This was another nonsense; Northern Ireland has always been treated differently from the rest of the UK.

Theresa May continued to insist that no British prime minister could ever agree to the EU's 'backstop' option for Northern Ireland, and to promise there would be no hard Irish border, while also insisting on leaving the EU customs union and avoiding a border in the Irish Sea. There was no elaboration on how these objectives were compatible, just vague talk of a 'highly streamlined customs arrangement', making use of technology to avoid laborious border checks, talk that was derided by the EU officials negotiating Brexit. One senior EU delegate maintained that vague talk of waivers for goods and services travelling over the border, or the UK collecting customs duties for the EU, or various untried technological solutions was 'a lot of magical thinking about how an invisible border would work in the future'.[24]

May had asserted after the referendum that there would be 'no return to the borders of the past'. But there was, it seemed, a return to the politics and ignorance of the past over the course of the next two years as a succession of clownish Tories revealed the depth of their ignorance and contempt when it came to Ireland, none more so than Boris Johnson, foreign secretary from July 2016 to July 2018, who embarrassingly suggested the invisible boundary between the London boroughs of Camden and Westminster as a possible model for a post-Brexit border. Johnson continued to dismiss the idea that the Irish border was a complicated issue and communicated his resentment at a private dinner in June 2018: 'it's so small and there are so few firms that actually use that border regularly it's just beyond belief that we're allowing the tail to wag the dog in this way. We're allowing the whole of our agenda to be dictated by this folly.'[25]

Another darling of the pro-Brexit backbenchers, Jacob Rees-Mogg, had suggested two months before the Brexit vote, 'There would be our ability, as we had during the Troubles, to have people inspected. It's not a border that everyone has to go through every day, but of course for security reasons during the Troubles, we kept a very close eye on the border, to try and stop gun-running and things like that.' He subsequently arrogantly insisted he had no reason to visit the Irish border to inform his views ('I don't think my visiting the border is really going to give me a fundamental insight into the border beyond what one can get by studying it'). He also suggested the British government should 'call Ireland's bluff' on the question of the border; Britain should claim it would not impose a border regardless of the outcome of Brexit negotiations: 'What would the Irish do if the EU insisted? I think that's a really interesting question. I think we should call that particular bluff.'[26] This was a moronic case of seeking to blame someone else for the consequences of Brexit and ignoring the reality of international trade rules, namely that if the UK left the EU trading bloc then a border would become an imperative.[27]

David Davis, Brexit secretary until July 2018, was forced to apologise for not telling Northern Ireland politicians about his first, farcical, visit to the Irish border, an unannounced trip to several sites along the County Armagh side of the border, almost two years after the Brexit referendum. There was still, it seemed, a determination to avoid, as former home secretary and prime minister James Callaghan was advised, 'getting sucked into the Irish bog'. Likewise, in March 2018 Theresa May walked through a farm between Bangor and Belfast in the constituency of North Down and looked indifferently at a cow, more than fifty miles away from the nearest section of the border. When asked whether she would be prepared to go to the border and see for herself the potential issues concerning people, May replied: 'My diary over the next year hasn't yet been set, but all I am saying is I understand ... I think it's not a question of just whether I actually go and stand on the Border, it's a question of do I understand the impact that it has for people?'[28]

There was something almost slapstick about this, akin to Spike Milligan's novel *Puckoon*, published in 1963. In an upstairs room at the Duke of Wellington Hotel in 1924: 'several high-ranking grim-faced boundary commissioners from both sides faced each other across a giant map of Ireland ... across the map, running left to right was a thick red pencil line that terminated just short of the Atlantic. It was the threatened new border. In its path lay sleeping Puckoon'. For ten days they had argued over the last few miles of frontier; one of them then decided it was time to be decisive: '"we only have this bit here to partition and the pubs close in an hour. Why not let's all put one hand on the red pencil and draw a line that falls naturally and peacefully into place?'" And so the fate of Puckoon was sealed; now to be divided by the border, with a customs shed on hallowed church ground.[29] In the aftermath of the Brexit vote the British government seemed to be taking the Irish border question as seriously as Milligan's boundary commissioners. Boris Johnson even toasted the British government's Chequers Agreement in July 2018 – a proposed 'common rulebook' with the EU post-Brexit for all goods, including agricultural produce, with Parliament having the option to 'diverge' from some rules and with 'different arrangements for services' – and then resigned over it.[30]

After the EU rejected the Chequers proposals in September 2018 Theresa May complained defiantly that she would not contemplate a deal that would 'divide our country' by treating Northern Ireland differently and threaten the 'integrity' of the UK. Similar protests about the division of Ireland had received short shrift a century previously. The 'backstop' of no checks and controls on any British border with the EU was also rejected by hardline Brexiteers, who introduced an amendment making it unlawful for Northern Ireland to be part of any customs territory outside of the UK. It was also argued that 'perversely, the backstop could ... be the thing that makes a harder border inevitable' because it was jeopardising the entire process.[31] Nor was it without irony that all the talk of a 'frictionless' border was causing much friction, and there were understandable fears expressed about the possibility of a reinstated 'hard' border becoming a target for violence as it had been at various stages during the twentieth century.

Following the Brexit referendum the DUP had rejected an invitation to cross the border to join a 'civic forum' convened by the Irish government and loudly insisted that the issues at stake were an internal British concern, ignoring that the very agreements it baulked at had allowed it to be the dominant party in the former power-sharing assembly. Those agreements were driven by the logic that Northern Ireland required special consideration and its constitutional arrangements needed to be worked out through partnership between North and South and London and Dublin. Arlene Foster later warned ominously of 'blood red' lines in relation to a special deal for Northern Ireland, persisting with the bombast that there could not be 'a differential between Northern Ireland and the rest of the UK' and suggesting the Belfast Agreement could also be altered.[32]

David Davis and Boris Johnson may have been vocal about the idea that the border issue was being exaggerated, but credible sources suggested otherwise. In 2018, the first officially agreed account since partition in 1920 – between the Republic's Department of Transport and the Northern Ireland Department for Infrastructure – revealed that Ireland had 208 border crossings and government technicians endured what was described as a 'nightmare' trying to map definitively all the roads, paths and dirt tracks that traverse the 500km of frontier, and there was still confusion about where the border juts in and out of routes, 'or where roads are privately owned on one side and publicly maintained on the other'. The border runs along the middle of eleven roads while it also meets in the middle of at least three bridges and dissects two ferry crossings. Significantly, 'there are more crossings in Ireland than along the entire border between the European Union and the countries to its east, which has 137'.[33] The uncertainty over Brexit also created the possibility it seemed, that small bridges erected to connect neighbours on both sides of the border could now become 'international links'.[34]

The border was not, insisted Darach MacDonald, just a logistical problem with economic consequences; culture, disrupted lives, history and sociology also had to be considered; because of its intrusions it was always a 'hard' border before the political and military situation improved.[35] Continuing that thread of thinking, Belfast-born actor Stephen Rea narrated a short film in September 2018, *Brexit: A Cry from the Irish Border*, in which he spoke of the border progress of the previous twenty years:

> roads that start here and end there, somehow allowing a wound to heal ... a gentleness in the mundanity ... daily travel across political lines; work, school, grocery shops, back again ... there, but not there; a line of imagination that needed imagination to make it exist while unseen ... we live here and we're holding our breath again.[36]

As they held their breath, in November 2018 the British government and the EU produced a draft agreement on British withdrawal from the EU. It included a protocol relating to Northern Ireland covering a backstop – in the event of the EU and UK failing to agree a deal on their future relationship by 31 December 2020 – to avoid a hard border in Ireland. This detailed that in the absence of a future deal, the whole of the UK would stay aligned with the EU customs union instead of just a specific rule applying to Northern Ireland as was originally proposed. The UK also agreed under the terms of this new backstop that Northern Ireland would remain aligned with a limited set of rules relating to the EU's single market.

In response, UK Brexit Secretary Dominic Rabb resigned and in his resignation letter to Theresa May complained that the agreement compromised the 'integrity' of the UK by indicating that Northern Ireland would need special arrangements in relation to post-Brexit trade.[37] This plaintiveness about the purity of the UK and distaste for specific arrangements for Northern Ireland flew in the face of the history of Northern Ireland and the

British, Irish and European relationships with it. Despite Raab's assertions, the reality was that Brexiteers, who offered no coherent alternative to the draft agreement, did not cherish Northern Ireland; rather it was a convenient tactic employed in a distinctly English power-game which also saw them cheering on the DUP in its trenchant opposition to the draft agreement. There was an element of history repeating itself, with some British Conservatives insisting on 'an extreme and dangerous strategy' as they had done in encouraging Ulster rebellion against home rule from 1910 to 1914 to try and gain the upper hand in domestic politics rather than because of a passion for Ireland.[38]

The irony was that the draft agreement seemed to provide Northern Ireland with 'the best of all worlds' economically, as was recognised by its business and farming communities whose views the DUP derided, as it did the wishes of the Northern Irish electorate, opting instead to bark its 'No Surrender' mantra, so practised over decades.[39]

Theresa May had travelled quite a road by altering her strategy of 'Brexit means Brexit' when faced with the prospect of no deal and therefore a hard exit from the EU. What she could not alter, however, was the parliamentary arithmetic. The Irish government looked on, happy that there had been remarkable unity among the other EU members about avoiding a hard Irish border and that its concerns had been addressed, but powerless to influence the balance of power in the House of Commons and the scale of the opposition to the draft agreement.

In the face of May's plight – how to avoid the backstop or indeed, end it if it came in to force was unclear as the UK would not be permitted to act unilaterally on this – the question remained whether the fear of a chaotic exit would outweigh the concerns of Brexiteers. What was certain, however, was that the border, as the Northern Ireland state approached its centenary, still had the capacity to polarise and frustrate, with reverberations well beyond Britain and Ireland.

The border question remained paramount, notwithstanding the contemptuous arrogance with which those who championed Brexit had treated the weight of Anglo-Irish history. Just after the draft EU–UK agreement, former UK Independence Party leader Nigel Farage was asked if he had ever considered Northern Ireland during the referendum campaign in 2016. Farage 'cheerfully' admitted he never gave it a moment's thought: 'No, no, no ... what's the problem? There is no problem'.[40]

Given the 'soft' or 'invisible' border arising out of the peace process and before Brexit, there was reason to believe that the 1955 reflections of Hubert Butler on the partition question were close to being vindicated. Butler had suggested that, in time, the border 'might become meaningless and drop off painlessly like a strip of plaster from a wound that had healed, or else survive in some modified form as a definition which distinguishes but does not divide'.[41] Brexit, however, rendered such optimism redundant and the bellicosity generated by the updated border debate inevitably brought a long history aggressively back into current affairs. Nonetheless, the reflections of Butler's generation of writers on the border remain profoundly relevant during the fraught Brexit era, including those of Benedict Kiely, born in Tyrone the year before the partition of Ireland. He maintained in 1945, 'the most that can be hoped for is that all Irishmen will some day learn to view the past without passion, to approach the present in the practical way that the artist or the craftsman approaches the material out of which he is to make something permanent and durable and essentially one'.[42]

That remains the challenge in order to lift the oppressive weight of a century of Anglo-Irish history.

Bibliography of Sources Cited

National Archives of Ireland

Dáil Éireann   Department of Foreign Affairs
Department of the Taoiseach

University College Dublin Archives

Papers of Éamon de Valera   Papers of Frank Aiken
Papers of Seán MacEntee   Papers of George Gavan Duffy

Newspapers

Belfast Newsletter   *Irish News*
Belfast Telegraph   *Irish Times*
Guardian   *Morning Post*
Independent   *Sunday Business Post*
Irish Examiner   *Sunday Times*
Irish Independent

Journals and Periodicals

Bullán: An Irish Studies Journal

Comparative Politics

Crane Bag

Foreign Affairs

History Ireland

Irish Economic and Social History

Irish Historical Studies

Irish Political Studies

Irish Studies in International Affairs

Irish Review

New Hibernia Review

Journal of Cross Border Studies

Past and Present

Political Geography

Studies

The Historical Journal

Reference Works

James Quinn and James McGuire (eds.), *A Dictionary of Irish Biography: From the Earliest Times to the Year 2002*, 9 vols. (Cambridge, 2009)

Official Reports and Publications

Dáil Éireann Debates

Seanad Éireann Debates

Books and Articles

Anderson, Malcolm and Eberhard Bort (eds.), *The Irish Border: History, Politics and Culture* (Liverpool, 1998)

Arthur, Paul, 'Anglo-Irish Relations and the Northern Ireland Problem', *Irish Studies in International Affairs* 2(1), 1985, pp. 37–50

Bardon, Jonathan, *A History of Ulster* (Belfast, 1992)

Barrington, Donal, 'Uniting Ireland', *Studies* 46(184) (Winter, 1957), pp. 379–402

Bartlett, Thomas, 'Ulster 1600–2000: Posing the Question', *Bullán: An Irish Studies Journal* 4(1) (Autumn 1998)

Bartlett, Thomas (ed.), *The Cambridge History of Ireland*, vol. IV: *1880 to the Present* (Cambridge, 2018)

Barton, Brian, 'Relations Between Westminster and Stormont', *Irish Political Studies* 7(1) (1992), pp. 1–20

Bew, Paul, '"The Blind Leading the Blind": London's Response to the 1969 Crisis', *History Ireland* 17(4) (July/August 2009), pp. 46–9
  Churchill and Ireland (Oxford, 2016)
  Ireland: The Politics of Enmity, 1789–2006 (Oxford, 2007)

Bew, Paul and John Bew, 'War and Peace in Northern Ireland, 1965–2016', in Bartlett (ed.), *Cambridge History of Ireland*, vol. IV, pp. 441–76

Bielenberg, Andy, 'Exodus: The Emigration of Southern Irish Protestants During the Irish War of Independence and Civil War', *Past and Present* 218 (February 2013), pp. 199–233

Bowman, John, *De Valera and the Ulster Question, 1917–73* (Oxford, 1982)

Browne, Noel, *Against the Tide* (Dublin, 1986)

Buckland, Patrick, *A History of Northern Ireland* (Dublin, 1981)

Buckland, Patrick (ed.), *Irish Unionism 1885–1923: A Documentary History* (Belfast, 1973)

Butler, Hubert, *Grandmother and Wolfe Tone* (Dublin, 1990)

Carr, Garrett, *The Rule of the Land: Walking Ireland's Border* (London, 2017)

Chambers, Anne, *T. K. Whitaker: Portrait of a Patriot* (Dublin, 2014)

Coakley, John, and Liam O'Dowd, 'The Transformation of the Irish Border', *Political Geography* 26 (2007), pp. 877–85

Connelly, Tony, *Brexit and Ireland: The Dangers, the Opportunities, and the Inside Story of the Irish Response* (Dublin, 2017)

Coogan, Tim Pat, *The IRA* (London, 1980)

Cronin, John Jeremiah and Pádraig Lenihan, 'Wars of Religion, 1641–1691', in Jane Ohlmeyer (ed.), *The Cambridge History of Ireland*, vol. III: *1550–1730* (Cambridge, 2018), pp. 246–73

Crowe, Catríona, Ronan Fanning, Michael Kennedy, Dermot Keogh, Eunan O'Halpin (eds.), *Documents on Irish Foreign Policy*, vols. II–X (Dublin, 2000–2016)

Cruise O'Brien, Conor, *Memoir: My Life and Themes* (Dublin, 2009)
  States of Ireland, 2nd edn (London, 1974)

d'Alton, Ian, 'A Protestant Paper for a Protestant People: The *Irish Times* and the Southern Irish Minority', *Irish Communications Review* 12 (2010), pp. 65–73

Daly, Mary E., 'Brexit and the Irish Border: Historical Context', A Royal
     Irish Academy/British Academy Brexit briefing, October 2017
de Fréine, Celia, 'On the Border of Memory: Childhood in a Divided
     Ireland', *New Hibernia Review* 8(1) (Spring 2004), pp. 9–20
de Paor, Liam, *Unfinished Business* (London, 1990)
Delaney, Paul, 'D. P. Moran and The Leader: Writing an Irish Ireland
     Through Partition', *Eire Ireland* 38(3/4) (Fall/Winter 2003), pp.
     189–211
Dooley, Terence, *The Plight of Monaghan Protestants, 1912–1926* (Dublin,
     2000)
Dunne, Tom 'RFF: A Writing Life', in Senia Paseta (ed.), *Uncertain
     Futures: Essays About the Irish Past for Roy Foster* (Oxford, 2016), pp.
     7–28
Dutton, David, *Austen Chamberlain: Gentleman in Politics* (London,
     1985)
Earner Byrne, Lindsey, 'The Family in Ireland, 1880–2015', in Bartlett
     (ed.), *Cambridge History of Ireland*, vol. IV, pp. 641–73
Ervine, St John, *Craigavon: Ulsterman* (London, 1949)
Fanning, Ronan, 'The British Dimension', *The Crane Bag* 8(1) (1984), pp.
     41–52
     Fatal Path: British Government and Irish Revolution, 1910–1922
          (London, 2013)
Farren, Seán, *The SDLP: The Struggle for Agreement in Northern Ireland,
     1970–2000* (Dublin, 2010)
Ferriter, Diarmaid, *Ambiguous Republic: Ireland in the 1970s* (London,
     2012)
     *Judging Dev: A Reassessment of the Life and Legacy of Éamon De
          Valera* (Dublin, 2007)
     Occasions of Sin: Sex and Society in Modern Ireland (London, 2009)
     The Transformation of Ireland, 1900–2000 (London, 2004)
Fisk, Robert, *In Time of War, Ireland, Ulster and the Price of Neutrality,
     1939–45* (London, 1983)
FitzGerald, Garret, *All in a Life: An Autobiography* (Dublin, 1991)
     Ireland and the World: Further Reflections (Dublin, 2005)
FitzGerald, John, and Edgar Morgenroth, 'The Northern Ireland
     Economy', Dublin Economics Workshop, 14 September 2018

Foster, Roy, *Luck and the Irish: A Brief History of Change* (London, 2007)

Fraser, T. G., *Partition in Ireland, India and Palestine: Theory and Practice* (London, 1984)

Freeman, T. W., *Ireland: Its Physical, Historical, Social and Economic Geography* (London, 1950)

Gibbons, Ivan, *The British Labour Party and the Establishment of the Irish Free State, 1918–1924* (London, 2015)

Gwynn, Denis, *The History of Partition, 1912–1925* (Dublin, 1950)

Hachey, Thomas (ed.), *The Problem of Partition: Peril to World Peace* (Chicago, 1972)

Hanley, Brian, and Scott Millar, *The Lost Revolution: The Story of the Official IRA and the Workers' Party* (Dublin, 2009)

Harkness, David, *Northern Ireland Since 1920* (Dublin, 1983)

Harris, Clodagh, 'Anglo-Irish Elite Co-Operation and the Peace Process: The Impact of the EEC/EU', *Irish Studies in International Affairs* 12 (2001), pp. 203–14

Hart, Peter, *Mick: The Real Michael Collins* (London, 2007)

Hassan, David, 'Sport, Identity, and the People of the Irish Border Lands', *New Hibernia Review*, 10(2) (Summer 2006), pp. 26–43

Healey, Denis, *The Time of My Life* (London, 1989)

Heaney, Seamus, *The Haw Lantern* (London, 1987)

    Opened Ground: Selected Poems, 1966–1996 (London, 1998)

    Preoccupations: Selected Prose, 1968–1978 (London, 1980)

Hennessey, Thomas, *A History of Northern Ireland* (London, 1997)

    Hunger Strike: Margaret Thatcher's Battle with the IRA, 1980–1981 (Dublin, 2014)

    The Northern Ireland Peace Process (Dublin, 2000)

Hepburn, A. C., *A Past Apart: Studies in the History of Catholic Belfast 1850–1950* (Belfast, 1996)

    The Conflict of Nationality in Modern Ireland (London, 1980)

Hughes, Brian, 'Loyalists and Loyalism in a Southern Irish Community, 1921–2', *Historical Journal*, 59(4) (December 2016), pp. 1075–1105

Hughes, Brian (ed.), *Eoin MacNeill: Memoir of a Revolutionary Scholar* (Dublin, 2016)

Humphreys, Richard, *Beyond the Border: The Good Friday Agreement and Irish Unity After Brexit* (Dublin, 2018)

Jackson, Alvin, *Ireland 1798–1998* (Oxford, 1999)

'Irish Unionism, 1905–21', in Peter Collins (ed.), *Conflict in Ireland, 1885–1921* (Belfast, 1994), pp. 45–7

'Unionist History', *Irish Review* 1(1) (Spring 1993), pp. 58–67

Johnson, D. S., 'Cattle Smuggling on the Irish Border, 1932–8', *Irish Economic and Social History* 6 (1979), pp. 41–64

Johnson, Thomas, *A Handbook for Rebels: A Guide to Successful Defiance of the British Government* (Dublin, 1918)

Kelly, Stephen, *'A failed political entity': Charles Haughey and the Northern Ireland Question, 1945–1992* (Dublin, 2016)

Fianna Fáil, Partition and Northern Ireland (Dublin, 2013)

Kennedy, Dennis, *The Widening Gulf: Northern Attitudes to the Independent Irish State, 1919–49* (Belfast, 1988)

Kennedy, Michael, *Division and Consensus: The Politics of Cross-Border Relations in Ireland 1925–69* (Dublin, 2000)

Keogh, Dermot *Jack Lynch: A Biography* (Dublin, 2008)

Kiely, Benedict, *Counties of Contention: A Study of the Origins and Implications of the Partition of Ireland* (Cork, 1945)

Laffan, Michael, *The Partition of Ireland, 1911–1925* (Dundalk, 1983)

Leary, Peter, *Unapproved Routes: Histories of the Irish Border, 1922–1972* (Oxford, 2016)

Lee, J. J., *Ireland, 1912–85: Politics and Society* (Cambridge, 1989)

Lewis, Geoffrey, *Carson: The Man Who Divided Ireland* (London, 2005)

Lynn, Brendan, 'Nationalist Politics in Derry, 1945–69', in Gerard O'Brien (ed.), *Derry and Londonderry: History and Society* (Dublin, 1999), pp. 604–25

Mac Cormaic, Ruadhán, *The Supreme Court: The Judges, the Decisions, the Rifts and the Rivalries That Have Shaped Ireland* (London, 2016)

Mac Suibhne, Breandán, and David Dickson (eds.), *The Outer Edge of Ulster: A Memoir of Social Life in 19th-Century Donegal* (Dublin 2000)

MacDonagh Oliver, *Ireland, the Union and Its Aftermath* (London, 1977)

MacDonald, Darach, *Hard Border: Walking Through a Century of Partition* (Dublin, 2018)

MacMaster, Norma, *Silence Under a Stone* (Dublin, 2017)

Matthews, Kevin, *Fatal Influence: The Impact of Ireland on British Politics, 1920–1925* (Dublin, 2004)

McCabe, Eugene, *Death and Nightingales* (London, 1992)
Heaven Lies About us (London, 2006 edn)

McCafferty, Nell, *Nell* (Dublin, 2004)

McKay, Susan, *Bear in Mind These Dead* (London, 2008)
Northern Protestants: An Unsettled People (Belfast, 2000)

McMahon, Paul, *British Spies and Irish Rebels: British Intelligence and Ireland, 1916–45* (Woodbridge, 2008)

Meehan, Elizabeth, "'Britain's Irish Question: Britain's European Question?': British–Irish Relations in the Context of European Union and the Belfast Agreement', *Review of International Studies* 26 (2000), pp. 83–97

Middlemas, Keith (ed.), *Thomas Jones: Whitehall Diary*, vol. III: *Ireland 1918–1925* (London, 1971)

Milligan, Spike, *Puckoon* (London, 1963)

Moloney, Ed, 'Censorship and the Troubles', in Mary Corcoran and Mark O'Brien (eds.), *Political Censorship and the Democratic State: The Irish Broadcasting Ban* (Dublin, 2005)

Montague, John, *The Pear is Ripe* (Dublin, 2007)

Moore, Christy, *One Voice: My Life in Song* (London, 2003)

Muldoon, Paul, *Why Brownlee Left* (London, 1980)

Mullin, Chris, *A Walk-on Part: Diaries 1994–1999* (London, 2012)

Mulroe, Patrick *Bombs, Bullets and the Border: Policing Ireland's Frontier: Irish Security Policy, 1969–1978* (Dublin, 2017)

Murray, Paul, *The Irish Boundary Commission and Its Origins, 1886–1925* (Dublin, 2011)
'Partition and the Irish Boundary Commission: A Northern Nationalist Perspective', *Clogher Record* 18(2), 2004, pp. 181–217

Nash, Catherine, 'Border Crossings: New Approaches to the Irish Border', *Irish Studies Review* 18(3) (2010), pp. 265–84

O Beacháin, Donnacha, *Destiny of the Soldiers: Fianna Fáil, Irish Republicanism and the IRA, 1926–73* (Dublin, 2010)

O Caoindealbháin, Brian, 'Citizenship and Borders: Irish Nationality Law and Northern Ireland', *Working papers in British-Irish Studies* no. 68 (2006), Institute for British-Irish Studies, University College Dublin

O Corráin, Daithí, '"Ireland in His Heart North and South": The Contribution of Ernest Blythe to the Partition Question', *Irish Historical Studies* 35(137) (May 2006), pp. 61–80

O'Brien, George, *The Four Green Fields* (Dublin, 1936)

O'Callaghan, Margaret, 'Old Parchment and Water: The Boundary Commission of 1925 and the Copper Fastening of the Irish Border', *Bullán, An Irish Studies Journal* 4(1) (1999/2000), pp. 27–55

O'Halloran, Clare, *Partition and the Limits of Irish Nationalism: An Ideology Under Stress* (Dublin, 1987)

O'Kane, Eamonn, 'Anglo-Irish Relations and the Northern Ireland Peace Process: From Exclusion to Inclusion', *Contemporary British History* 18(1) (Spring 2004), pp. 78–99

O'Neill, David, *The Partition of Ireland: How and Why It Was Accomplished* (Dublin, 1949)

O'Rawe, Richard, *Blanketmen: An Untold Story of the H-Block Hunger Strike* (Dublin, 2005)

Ó Tuathaigh, Gearóid, 'Ireland 1880–2016: Negotiating Sovereignty and Freedom', in Tom Bartlett (ed.), *The Cambridge History of Ireland*, vol. IV: *1880 to the Present* (Cambridge, 2018), pp. 1–33

Patterson, Henry, *Ireland Since 1939: The Persistence of Conflict* (Dublin, 2006)

Peck, John, *Dublin from Downing Street* (Dublin, 1978)

Perry, Nicholas, 'The Irish Landed Class and the British Army, 1850–1950', *War in History* 18(3) (2011), pp. 304–32

Phoenix, Eamon, *Northern Nationalism: Nationalist Politics, Partition and the Catholic Minority in Northern Ireland 1890–1940* (Belfast, 1994)

Pollak, Andy, 'Interview on North-South Cooperation with the Taoiseach, Brian Cowen TD', *Journal of Cross Border Studies in Ireland* 5 (Spring 2010), pp. 11–20

Power, Paul F., '"The Anglo-Irish Problem: A Matter of Which Question', *Comparative Politics* 26(12) (January 1994), pp. 237–50

Ralaheen Ltd Dublin, with EXPAC Monaghan and Strategem Belfast, *All Over the Place: People Displaced to and from the Southern Border Counties as a Result of the Conflict* (Monaghan, 2005)

Rees, Merlyn, *Northern Ireland: A Personal Perspective* (London, 1985)

Rouse, Paul, *Sport and Ireland: A History* (Oxford, 2015)

Routledge, Paul, *John Hume* (London, 1998)

Savage, Robert, *A Loss of Innocence? Television and Irish Society, 1960–1972* (Manchester, 2010)

Shannon, William V., 'The Anglo-Irish Agreement', *Foreign Affairs* 64(4) (Spring 1986), pp. 849–70

Sheehy, Michael, *Divided We Stand: A Study of Partition* (London, 1955)

Smith, Jeremy, *The Tories and Ireland, 1910–1914: Conservative Party Politics and the Home Rule Crisis* (Dublin, 2000)

Sweetman, Rosita, *On Our Backs: Sexual Attitudes in a Changing Ireland* (London, 1979)

Taylor, A. J. P., *English History 1914–1945* (Oxford, 1965)

Tóibín, Colm, *Walking Along the Border* (London, 1987)

Travers, Stephen, and Neil Featherstonehaugh, *The Miami Showband Massacre: A Survivor's Search for the Truth* (Dublin, 2007)

Treacy, Matt, *The IRA, 1956–69: Rethinking the Republic* (Manchester, 2011)

Trevor, William, *Collected Stories* (London, 1993)

Walsh, John, *Patrick Hillery: The Official Biography* (Dublin, 2008)

Whyte, John H., *Interpreting Northern Ireland* (Oxford, 1990)

Wilson, Harold, *Final Term: The Labour Government, 1974–6* (London 1979)

Wilson, Tom, *Ulster: Conflict and Consent* (London, 1989)

Wright, Nicholas, 'Brexit and Ireland: Collateral Damage?', in Benjamin Martill and Uta Staiger (eds.), *Brexit and Beyond* (London, 2018), pp. 105–13

Notes

1: The Long Gestation

1. Thomas Bartlett, 'Ulster 1600–2000: Posing the Question', *Bullán: An Irish Studies Journal* 4(1) (Autumn 1998), pp. 5–19.
2. Ibid.
3. Michael Laffan, *The Partition of Ireland, 1911–1925* (Dundalk, 1983), p. 2.
4. Ibid. and Malcolm Anderson and Eberhard Bort (eds.), *The Irish Border: History, Politics and Culture* (Liverpool, 1998).
5. Laffan, *Partition of Ireland*, p. 107.
6. *The Home Rule Instalment Bill and Its Rejection by Home Rulers: Publications of the Irish Unionist Alliance Before and After* (Dublin, 1907).
7. Oliver MacDonagh, *Ireland, the Union and Its Aftermath* (London, 1977), p. 16.
8. St John Ervine, *Craigavon: Ulsterman* (London, 1949), p. 32.
9. Laffan, *Partition of Ireland*, p. 38.
10. Eamon Phoenix, *Northern Nationalism: Nationalist Politics, Partition and the Catholic Minority in Northern Ireland 1890–1940* (Belfast, 1994), pp. 29–35.
11. Geoffrey Lewis, *Carson: The Man Who Divided Ireland* (London, 2005), pp. 214–15.

12. Ronan Fanning, *Fatal Path: British Government and Irish Revolution, 1910–1922* (London, 2013).

13. Laffan, *Partition of Ireland*, p. 62.

14. Fanning, *Fatal Path*, p. 207.

15. Ibid.

16. Ibid.

17. Ibid., p. 212.

18. Ibid., pp. 211–12.

19. Laffan, *Partition of Ireland*, p. 61.

20. Fanning, *Fatal Path*, p. 219.

21. David Harkness, *Northern Ireland Since 1920* (Dublin, 1983), p. 6.

22. T. W. Freeman, *Ireland: Its Physical, Historical, Social and Economic Geography* (London, 1950) p. 495.

23. D. S. Johnson, 'Cattle Smuggling on the Irish Border, 1932–8', *Irish Economic and Social History* 6 (1979), pp. 41–64.

24. Ibid.

25. Ibid.

26. David O'Neill, *The Partition of Ireland: How and Why It Was Accomplished* (Dublin, 1949), p. 3.

27. Denis Gwynn, *The History of Partition, 1912–1925* (Dublin, 1950), p. 84.

28. Alvin Jackson, 'Irish Unionism, 1905–21', in Peter Collins (ed.), *Conflict in Ireland, 1885–1921* (Belfast, 1994), pp. 45–7, and Thomas Johnson, *A Handbook for Rebels: A Guide to Successful Defiance of the British Government* (Dublin, 1918).

29. Dennis Kennedy, *The Widening Gulf: Northern Attitudes to the Independent Irish State, 1919–49* (Belfast, 1988), p. 58.

30. Patrick Buckland (ed.), *Irish Unionism 1885–1923: A Documentary History* (Belfast, 1973), p. 410.

31. Thomas Hennessey, *A History of Northern Ireland* (London, 1997), p. 11.

32. Keith Middlemas (ed.), *Thomas Jones: Whitehall Diary*, vol. III: *Ireland 1918–1925* (London, 1971), pp. xi–xvii.

33. Ibid., p. 93, 7 September 1921.

34. Ibid. p. 160, 10 November 1921, and Margaret O'Callaghan, 'Old Parchment and Water: The Boundary Commission of 1925 and the

Copper Fastening of the Irish Border', *Bullán, An Irish Studies Journal* 4(1) (1999/2000), pp. 27–55.

35. Fanning, *Fatal Path*, p. 214.

36. Middlemas (ed.), *Jones: Whitehall Diary*, p. 110, 14 October 1921.

37. Ibid., p. 147, 7 November 1921.

38. Paul Murray, *The Irish Boundary Commission and Its Origins, 1886–1925* (Dublin, 2011), pp. 304ff.

39. O'Callaghan, 'Old Parchment and Water'.

40. Middlemas (ed.), *Jones: Whitehall Diary*, pp. xviii–xx.

41. Ibid., p. 110, 30 July 1921.

42. Ibid., pp. 163–4, 7 November 1921.

43. Ibid., p. 178, 5 December 1921.

44. Ibid., p. 181, 6 December 1921.

45. Peter Hart, *Mick: The Real Michael Collins* (London, 2007), p. 367.

46. National Archives of Ireland (hereafter NAI) Dáil Eireann (hereafter DE) 2/304/1, Craig to Lloyd George, 14 December 1921.

47. Paul McMahon, *British Spies and Irish Rebels: British Intelligence and Ireland, 1916–45* (Woodbridge, 2008), pp. 134–62.

48. O'Callaghan 'Old Parchment and Water', p. 37.

49. Kevin Matthews, *Fatal Influence: The Impact of Ireland on British Politics, 1920–1925* (Dublin, 2004), p. 189.

50. Lewis, *Carson*, pp. 231–2.

51. A. J. P. Taylor, *English History 1914–1945* (Oxford, 1965), pp. 161 and 236; Charles Townshend, 'The Irish War of Independence: Context and Meaning', in Catríona Crowe (ed.), *Guide to the Military Service (1916–23) Pensions Collection* (Dublin, 2012), pp. 110–24.

52. David Dutton, *Austen Chamberlain: Gentleman in Politics* (London, 1985), p. 167.

53. James Quinn, 'John (Jack) Beattie', in James Quinn and James McGuire (eds.), *A Dictionary of Irish Biography: From the Earliest Times to the Year 2002* (hereafter *DIB*), 9 vols. (Cambridge, 2009) I, p. 390.

54. Ivan Gibbons, *The British Labour Party and the Establishment of the Irish Free State, 1918–1924* (London, 2015), pp. 79–114.

55. Ibid.

56. NAI Department of the Taoiseach (hereafter DT) S11209, 'Deputation from Northern Ireland to the Provisional Government', 11 October 1922.
57. NAI DT S5750/2, 25 January 1923.

2: An Entrenched Partition

1. Phoenix, *Northern Nationalism*, pp. 288–337.
2. Ibid., p. 237.
3. A. C. Hepburn, *A Past Apart: Studies in the History of Catholic Belfast 1850–1950* (Belfast, 1996), pp. 120–27.
4. Phoenix, *Northern Nationalism*, p. 356.
5. Patrick Buckland, *A History of Northern Ireland* (Dublin, 1981), p. 67.
6. Norma MacMaster, *Silence Under a Stone* (Dublin, 2017).
7. Brian Hughes, 'Loyalists and Loyalism in a southern Irish community, 1921–2', *Historical Journal* 59(4) (December 2016), pp. 1075–1105.
8. Ibid. and Nicholas Perry, 'The Irish Landed Class and the British Army, 1850–1950', *War in History* 18(3) (2011), pp. 304–32.
9. Andy Bielenberg, 'Exodus: The Emigration of Southern Irish Protestants During the Irish War of Independence and Civil War', *Past and Present* 218 (February 2013), pp. 199–233.
10. Ibid., p. 232.
11. Ian d'Alton, 'A Protestant Paper for a Protestant People: The *Irish Times* and the Southern Irish Minority', *Irish Communications Review* 12 (2010), p. 65.
12. Ibid.
13. Ibid.
14. Tom Dunne, 'RFF: A Writing Life', in Senia Paseta (ed.), *Uncertain Futures: Essays About the Irish Past for Roy Foster* (Oxford, 2016), pp. 7–28.
15. Terence Dooley, *The Plight of Monaghan Protestants, 1912–1926* (Dublin, 2000), pp. 57–8.
16. Hughes, 'Loyalists and Loyalism'.

17. Gearóid Ó Tuathaigh, 'Ireland 1880–2016: Negotiating Sovereignty and Freedom', in Tom Bartlett (ed.), *The Cambridge History of Ireland*, vol. IV: *1880 to the Present* (Cambridge, 2018), pp. 1–33.

18. Breandán Mac Suibhne and David Dickson (eds.), *The Outer Edge of Ulster: A Memoir of Social Life in 19th-Century Donegal* (Dublin 2000), pp. 1–6.

19. *Irish Times*, 2 April 1923.

20. Ibid.

21. Cited in Gibbons, *The British Labour Party*, p. 171.

22. NAI DT S4743, Memorandum by Kevin O'Shiel on North Eastern Boundary Bureau, 14 October 1922.

23. University College Dublin Archives (UCDA) P152/261–74, Papers of George Gavan Duffy, Duffy to 'Fr H', 15 March 1922.

24. NAI DT S4743, Memorandum by Kevin O'Shiel on North Eastern Boundary Bureau, 14 October 1922.

25. NAI DT S2027, Memorandum from Kevin O'Shiel to the cabinet, 30 May 1923.

26. Ibid.

27. NAI DT S4084, North-Eastern Boundary Bureau: Memorandum from Kevin O'Higgins to the cabinet, 25 September 1924.

28. Ibid.

29. O'Callaghan, 'Old Parchment and Water'.

30. Ibid.

31. Thomas Hachey (ed.), *The Problem of Partition: Peril to World Peace* (Chicago, 1972), p. xiii; T. G. Fraser, *Partition in Ireland, India and Palestine: Theory and Practice* (London, 1984), p. 13.

32. Fraser, *Partition in Ireland*, pp. 15–19.

33. Ibid., pp. 194–6.

34. Paul F. Power, 'The Anglo-Irish Problem: A Matter of Which Question', *Comparative Politics* 26(12) (January 1994), pp. 237–50.

35. Peter Leary, *Unapproved Routes: Histories of the Irish Border, 1922–1972* (Oxford, 2016), pp. 54–5.

36. Lewis, *Carson*, p. 233.

37. Paul Muldoon, *Why Brownlee Left* (London, 1980), p. 15.

38. Alvin Jackson, 'Unionist History', *Irish Review* 1(1) (Spring 1993), pp. 58–67.

39. O'Callaghan, 'Old Parchment and Water', p. 38.
40. Ibid.
41. Donald R. Pearce (ed.), *The Senate Speeches of W. B. Yeats* (London, 2001 edn), p. 76.
42. Murray, *The Irish Boundary Commission*, pp. 129–30.
43. Ibid., pp. 105–7.
44. Paul Murray, 'Partition and the Irish Boundary Commission: A Northern Nationalist Perspective', *Clogher Record* 18(2), 2004, pp. 181–217.
45. Cahir Healy to editor of *Irish Independent*, 30 November 1925, cited in Eamon Phoenix, 'Cahir Healy', *DIB*, IV, pp. 555–8.
46. *Belfast News Letter*, 7 December 1925.
47. Brian Hughes (ed.), *Eoin MacNeill: Memoir of a Revolutionary Scholar* (Dublin, 2016), pp. 20–21.
48. A. C. Hepburn, *The Conflict of Nationality in Modern Ireland* (London, 1980), p. 165.
49. Kennedy, *The Widening Gulf*, pp. 228–9.
50. Ibid.
51. Paul Delaney, 'D. P. Moran and The Leader: Writing an Irish Ireland Through Partition', *Eire Ireland* 38(3/4) (Fall/Winter 2003), pp. 189–211.
52. Ibid. and Clare O'Halloran, *Partition and the Limits of Irish Nationalism: An Ideology Under Stress* (Dublin, 1987), pp. 1–27 and 97–131.
53. Ibid.
54. Daithí Ó Corráin, '"Ireland in His Heart North and South": The Contribution of Ernest Blythe to the Partition Question', *Irish Historical Studies* 35(137) (May 2006), pp. 61–80.
55. Patrick Lynch, 'George O'Brien', *DIB*, vol. VII, pp. 39–42.
56. George O'Brien, *The Four Green Fields* (Dublin, 1936), pp. 126–7.
57. Laffan, *Partition of Ireland*, p. 121.
58. Stephen Kelly, *Fianna Fáil, Partition and Northern Ireland* (Dublin, 2013), pp. 24–49.
59. NAI DT S10864, Note by Éamon de Valera of meeting with Sir Alexander Maguire, 5 February 1935, in Catríona Crowe, Ronan Fanning, Michael Kennedy, Dermot Keogh, Eunan O'Halpin (eds.),

Documents on Irish Foreign Policy (hereafter *DIFP*), vol. IV (Dublin, 2004), p. 334.

60. Diarmaid Ferriter, *Judging Dev: A Reassessment of the Life and Legacy of Éamon De Valera* (Dublin, 2007), p. 150.

61. Mary E. Daly, 'Brexit and the Irish Border: Historical Context', A Royal Irish Academy/British Academy Brexit briefing, October 2017; www.ria.ie/news/policy-and-international-relations/ria-british-academy-brexit-briefing-paper-series, accessed 20 November 2018.

62. Johnson, 'Cattle Smuggling on the Irish Border'.

63. Ibid.

64. Ibid.

65. Bowman, John, *De Valera and the Ulster Question, 1917–73* (Oxford, 1982), p. 308.

66. UCDA P67/155, Papers of Seán MacEntee, Draft letter from Seán MacEntee to Éamon de Valera, 17 February 1938.

67. UCDA P150/2179, John W. Dulanty to Joseph Walshe, 9 May 1934, in *DIFP*, vol. IV, p. 285, and Dulanty to Walshe 15 September 1936, ibid., p. 476.

68. Walshe to De Valera, 2 May 1936, ibid., pp. 434–5.

69. Paul Bew, *Churchill and Ireland* (Oxford, 2016), p. 147.

70. Ibid., pp. 156–8.

71. UCDA P150/2548, Item 11, 26 June 1940.

72. J. J. Lee, *Ireland, 1912–85: Politics and Society* (Cambridge, 1989), p. 223.

73. Bew, *Churchill and Ireland*, and *Irish Times*, 30 April 2018.

74. *Irish Times*, 31 March 1944.

75. Robert Fisk, *In Time of War: Ireland, Ulster and the Price of Neutrality, 1939–45* (London, 1983), p. 469.

76. Jonathan Bardon, *A History of Ulster* (Belfast, 1992), p. 554.

77. Article by Conor McMahon, 22 January 2017; www.thejournal.ie/cross-border-customs-ireland-2–3197617-Jan2017/, accessed 30 April 2018.

78. *Belfast Telegraph*, 19 December 1939, quoted in Philip Ollerenshaw, 'Neutrality and Belligerence: Ireland 1939–45', in Bartlett (ed.), *Cambridge History of Ireland*, vol. IV, pp. 349–81.

79. Quoted in Garret FitzGerald, *Ireland and the World: Further Reflections* (Dublin, 2005), p. 84.

80. Bowman, *De Valera and the Ulster Question*, p. 308; F. S. L. Lyons, 'De Valera Revisited', *Magill*, March 1981, p. 60.

81. Kelly, *Fianna Fáil, Partition and Northern Ireland*, p. 126.

82. Brian Walker, 'Pushing the Irish Unity agenda could backfire on the South', *Irish Times*, 28 August 2017.

83. Brendan Lynn, 'Nationalist Politics in Derry, 1945–69', in Gerard O'Brien (ed.), *Derry and Londonderry: History and Society* (Dublin, 1999), pp. 604–25.

84. Ibid.

85. Benedict Kiely, *Counties of Contention: A Study of the Origins and Implications of the Partition of Ireland* (Cork, 1945), pp. 1–2.

86. Ibid. and Patrick Maume, 'Benedict (Ben) Kiely', added to *DIB* online, June 2013; www.dib.cambridge.org, accessed 15 October 2018.

87. Kiely, *Counties of Contention*, p. 184.

88. *Irish Times*, 2 June 1945.

89. Quoted in *Irish Times*, 18 September 1969.

90. Brian Barton, 'Relations Between Westminster and Stormont', *Irish Political Studies* 7(1) (1992), p. 12.

91. Ibid.

92. Bardon, *History of Ulster*, pp. 601–2.

93. NAI Department of Foreign Affairs (hereafter DFA) 10/P/203/2, 'Labour Leaders and Partition', draft confidential report by Con Cremin, 13 December 1956, *DIFP*, vol. X, pp. 704–6.

94. NAI DFA/14/67, Holy See Embassy, Seán MacBride to Lord Jowitt, 4 October 1948, *DIFP*, vol. IX, pp. 182–4.

95. Dublin Diocesan Archives AB8/B/XVIII/52/2, Seán MacBride to Frank Pakenham, 1 March 1949, *DIFP*, vol. IX, pp. 333.

96. Ibid.

97. NAI DFA/10/P203, F. H. Boland to Sean Nunan, 6 June 1951, *DIFP*, vol. IX, pp. 667–9.

98. NAI DFA F/132/1/2, London Embassy, F. H. Boland to Tim O'Driscoll, 26 September 1951, *DIFP*, vol. X, pp. 61–2.

99. Paul Arthur, 'Anglo-Irish Relations and the Northern Ireland Problem', *Irish Studies in International Affairs* 2(1), 1985, pp. 37–50.

100. NAI DFA/5/305/14/243, F. H. Boland to Seán Nunan, 2 October 1954, *DIFP*, vol. X, pp. 418–21.

3: Old Fantasies, New Perspectives and a Gentle Thaw

1. UCDA P104/5805, Papers of Frank Aiken, Secret memorandum by Frank Aiken, 5 July 1951, *DIFP*, vol. X, pp. 14–15.
2. UCDA P104/8037, Memorandum by Frank Aiken of meeting with Lord Salisbury, 28 October 1952, *DIFP*, vol. X, p. 188.
3. NAI DFA/10/P/250, Conor Cruise O'Brien to Joseph Brennan, 3 August 1954, *DIFP*, vol. X, pp. 386–7.
4. Ibid.
5. NAI DFA/10/P12/6, Joseph Brennan to Leo McAuley, 28 October 1948, *DIFP*, vol. IX, p. 206.
6. NAI DFA/A/5/305/134/A, John J. Hearne to F. H. Boland, 11 July 1950, ibid., p. 578.
7. NAI/DFA/5/305/12/134/3, Memorandum by John J. Hearne, 8 September 1951, *DIFP*, vol. X, pp. 45–6.
8. Ibid.
9. NAI/DFA/10/P/277/2, Memorandum for government by John A. Costello, 30 April 1956, *DIFP*, vol. X, pp. 576–7.
10. NAI DFA/10/P/271/1, Report on visit to Six Counties by Mr Belton and Dr Mac White, 20–23 September 1955, ibid., p. 502.
11. *Irish News*, 15 November 1954.
12. Eamon Phoenix, 'Edward Gerard (Eddie) McAteer', *DIB*, vol. V, pp. 716–19.
13. www.irishsongs.com/lyrics.php?Action=view&Song_id=193. Accessed 24 October 2018.
14. Seanad Eireann Debates, 44, 24 November 1954.
15. Ibid., 25 November 1954.
16. Quoted in Lindsey Earner Byrne, 'The Family in Ireland, 1880–2015', in Bartlett (ed.), *Cambridge History of Ireland*, vol. IV, pp. 641–73.
17. Noel Browne, *Against the Tide* (Dublin, 1986), pp. 169–70.
18. Earner Byrne, 'The Family in Ireland'.
19. Ibid.

20. Lawrence William White, 'Seán (Sabhat) South', *DIB*, vol. VIII, pp. 1078–9.

21. www.irishsongs.com/lyrics.php?Action=view&Song_id=292. Accessed 9 November 2018.

22. Brian Hanley and Scott Millar, *The Lost Revolution: The Story of the Official IRA and the Workers' Party* (Dublin, 2009), pp. 1–22.

23. Matt Treacy, *The IRA, 1956–69: Rethinking the Republic* (Manchester, 2011), pp. 12, 125.

24. Ibid., p. 36.

25. Tim Pat Coogan, *The IRA* (London, 1980), p. 418.

26. Hubert Butler, 'Crossing the Border' (1955), in *Grandmother and Wolfe Tone* (Dublin, 1990) pp. 64–9.

27. Ó Corráin, '"Ireland in his Heart, North and South"'.

28. Michael Sheehy, *Divided We Stand: A Study of Partition* (London, 1955), p. 19.

29. Donal Barrington, 'Uniting Ireland', *Studies* 46(184) (Winter, 1957), pp. 379–402.

30. Ruadhán Mac Cormaic, *The Supreme Court: The Judges, the Decisions, the Rifts and the Rivalries That Have Shaped Ireland* (London, 2016), p. 118.

31. Leary, *Unapproved Routes*, pp. 62–86.

32. Celia de Fréine, 'On the Border of Memory: Childhood in a Divided Ireland', *New Hibernia Review* 8(1) (Spring 2004), pp. 9–20.

33. Ibid.

34. Diarmaid Ferriter, 'John Francis D'Alton', *DIB*, vol. III, pp. 11–13.

35. *Irish Times*, 2 February 1963.

36. *Irish Times*, 4 March 1957.

37. Ibid.

38. *Irish Times*, 5 March 1957.

39. *Irish Times*, 25 January 1965.

40. Ronan Fanning, 'Seán Lemass', *DIB*, vol. V, pp. 433–44.

41. Joe Lee, 'Lemass: His two partnerships', *Irish Times*, 19 May 1976.

42. Quoted in Henry Patterson, *Ireland Since 1939: The Persistence of Conflict* (Dublin, 2006), pp. 149–50.

43. John FitzGerald, 'Agriculture, Taxes and Northern Ireland: The Brexit talks echoes of times past', *Irish Times*, 27 April 2018.

44. Robert Savage, *A Loss of Innocence? Television and Irish Society, 1960–1972* (Manchester, 2010), p. 238.
45. Quoted in Stephen Kelly, *'A Failed Political Entity': Charles Haughey and the Northern Ireland Question, 1945–1992* (Dublin, 2016), p. xvi.
46. John Hume 'The Northern Catholic', parts I and II, *Irish Times*, 18 and 19 May 1964.
47. Lynn, 'Nationalist Politics in Derry, 1945–69'.
48. *Irish Times* 15 October 1974.
49. William Trevor, 'The Distant Past', in *Collected Stories* (London, 1993), pp. 349–57.
50. Ibid.

4: Violence and Containment

1. Patrick Maume, 'Patrick John Hillery', *DIB* online entry added June 2014, www.dib.cambridge.org, accessed 8 October 2018, and John Walsh, *Patrick Hillery: The Official Biography* (Dublin, 2008), pp. 191–5.
2. Michael Kennedy, *Division and Consensus: The Politics of Cross-Border Relations in Ireland 1925–69* (Dublin, 2000), pp. 332–68.
3. Ronan Fanning, 'John Mary ("Jack") Lynch', *DIB*, vol. V, pp. 630–41.
4. Michael Heney, 'Unresolved Aspects of the 1970 Arms Crisis', PhD thesis, University College Dublin, 2017, pp. 159–92.
5. Dermot Keogh, *Jack Lynch: A Biography* (Dublin, 2008), p. 229.
6. Ibid., pp. 209–11, and Anne Chambers, *T. K. Whitaker: Portrait of a Patriot* (Dublin, 2014).
7. Chambers, *T. K. Whitaker*, pp. 285–90.
8. Donnacha Ó Beacháin, *Destiny of the Soldiers: Fianna Fáil, Irish Republicanism and the IRA, 1926–73* (Dublin, 2010), p. 301.
9. Paul Bew, *Ireland: The Politics of Enmity, 1789–2006* (Oxford, 2007), pp. 489–501.
10. Kelly, *Fianna Fáil, Partition and Northern Ireland*, p. 6.
11. Ralaheen Ltd Dublin, with EXPAC Monaghan and Strategem Belfast, *All Over the Place: People Displaced to and from the Southern*

Border Counties as a Result of the Conflict (Monaghan, 2005), pp. 34–5.

12. Jonathan Bardon, 'Trimble's toughest task', *Irish Times*, 25 May 1998.

13. Paul Bew, '"The Blind Leading the Blind": London's Response to the 1969 Crisis', *History Ireland* 17(4) (July/August 2009), pp. 46–9.

14. Ibid.

15. Denis Healey, *The Time of My Life* (London, 1989), pp. 342–3.

16. Seán Farren, *The SDLP: The Struggle for Agreement in Northern Ireland, 1970–2000* (Dublin, 2010), p. 66.

17. Eamonn McCann, 'Bloody Sunday helped reconcile southern nationalists to Partition', *Irish Times*, 28 January 2012.

18. NAI DT 2002/8/489, Note of discussion between Jack Lynch and Edward Heath, 6 December 1971.

19. NAI DT 2002/8/847, Discussions between Jack Lynch and Edward Heath, 5 September 1972, and Jack Lynch note of talks with Heath, 23 October 1972.

20. Bew, *Ireland*, pp. 509–10.

21. Lee, *Ireland, 1912–58*, p. 434.

22. As quoted in *Irish Times*, 19 July 2005.

23. Ibid.

24. Quoted in Clodagh Harris: 'Anglo-Irish Elite Co-Operation and the Peace Process: The Impact of the EEC/EU', *Irish Studies in International Affairs* 12 (2001), pp. 203–14.

25. Diarmaid Ferriter, *Ambiguous Republic: Ireland in the 1970s* (London, 2012), p. 389.

26. Daly, 'Brexit and the Irish Border'.

27. Garrett Carr, *The Rule of the Land: Walking Ireland's Border* (London, 2017), p. 77.

28. *Irish Times*, 9 March 1973.

29. Ibid.

30. Conor Cruise O'Brien, *Memoir: My Life and Themes* (Dublin, 2009), p. 341.

31. Conor Cruise O'Brien, *States of Ireland*, 2nd edn (London, 1974), p. 276.

32. *Irish Times*, 9 October 1972.

33. NAI DT 2004/21/466, Note of discussion with Prof. Richard Conroy and James Prior, 22 February 1973.

34. NAI DT 2004/21/670, Notes of meeting between Irish government and the SDLP, 12 July 1973.

35. NAI DT 2004/21/670, Draft letter of Cosgrave to Gerry Fitt, July 1973.

36. NAI DT 2005/145/2569, Notes of meeting between Seán Donlon and the SDLP, 29 October 1973.

37. Ferriter, *Ambiguous Republic*, pp. 168–80.

38. Ibid., p. 178.

39. Diarmaid Ferriter and Patrick Maume, 'William (Billy) Fox', *DIB*, vol. III, pp. 1086–7.

40. Seamus Heaney, *Preoccupations: Selected Prose, 1968–1978* (London, 1980), p. 35.

41. Seamus Heaney, 'Terminus', in *Opened Ground: Selected Poems, 1966–1996* (London, 1998), pp. 295–6.

42. Seamus Heaney, 'From the Frontier of Writing', in *The Haw Lantern* (London, 1987), p. 6.

43. Harold Wilson, *Final Term: The Labour Government, 1974–6* (London 1979), p. 66.

44. Ibid., p. 74.

45. Ibid., p. 77.

46. Bardon, *History of Ulster*, p. 712.

47. Merlyn Rees, *Northern Ireland: A Personal Perspective* (London, 1985), pp. 273–4.

48. NAI DT 2005/7/649, Northern Ireland: Relations with the SDLP, January 1974 to August 1975.

49. *Irish Times*, 31 August 1977.

50. John Peck, *Dublin from Downing Street* (Dublin, 1978), pp. 123–5.

51. Darach MacDonald, *Hard Border: Walking Through a Century of Partition* (Dublin, 2018), p. 8.

52. Leary, *Unapproved Routes*, pp. 177–207.

53. Carr, *Rule of the Land*, p. 48.

54. Susan McKay, *Northern Protestants: An Unsettled People* (Belfast, 2000), p. 190.

55. NAI DT 2008/148/689, Partition, Marie Hetherington to Jack Lynch, 11 March 1978.

56. Carr, *Rule of the Land*, pp. 69–75.

57. John Montague, *The Pear is Ripe* (Dublin, 2007), p. 127.

58. Nell McCafferty, *Nell* (Dublin, 2004), pp. 147–50.

59. Susan McKay, *Bear in Mind These Dead* (London, 2008), p. 3.

60. Rosita Sweetman, *On Our Backs: Sexual Attitudes in a Changing Ireland* (London, 1979), p. 156.

61. McCafferty, *Nell*, pp. 221–7.

62. Peck, *Dublin from Downing Street*, pp. 124–5.

63. NAI DT 2005/7/587, Liam Cosgrave to Robin Glassock, 25 March 1973.

64. NAI DT 2007/116/742, IRA activities in Ireland, Liam Cosgrave to D. L. Armstrong, 9 February 1977.

65. Peck, *Dublin from Downing Street*, pp. 124–5.

66. Patrick Mulroe, *Bombs, Bullets and the Border: Policing Ireland's Frontier: Irish Security Policy, 1969–1978* (Dublin, 2017), pp. 55–95.

67. Ibid.

68. *Sunday Business Post*, 18 December 2011; *Irish Times*, 12 July 2006; Stephen Travers and Neil Featherstonehaugh, *The Miami Showband Massacre: A Survivor's Search for the Truth* (Dublin, 2007).

69. Leary, *Unapproved Routes*, p. 96.

70. Paul Rouse, *Sport and Ireland: A History* (Oxford, 2015), p. 242.

71. Ibid., pp. 267–9.

72. Ibid., p. 264.

73. Ibid., pp. 256–300.

74. David Hassan, 'Sport, Identity, and the People of the Irish Border Lands', *New Hibernia Review*, 10(2) (Summer 2006), pp. 26–43.

75. Ibid.

76. Ibid.

5: Kinks, Wiggles and Diplomacy

1. Ronan Fanning, 'The British Dimension', *The Crane Bag* 8(1) (1984), pp. 41–52.

2. Thomas Hennessey, *The Northern Ireland Peace Process* (Dublin, 2000), p. 22.
3. Kelly, *'A Failed Political Entity'*, pp. 41ff.
4. Ibid., pp. 352–3.
5. Thomas Hennessey, *Hunger Strike: Margaret Thatcher's battle with the IRA, 1980–1981* (Dublin, 2014).
6. *Irish Times*, 11 January 2014.
7. Richard O'Rawe, *Blanketmen: An Untold Story of the H-Block Hunger Strike* (Dublin, 2005), p. 153.
8. Christy Moore, *One Voice: My Life in Song* (London, 2003), p. 89.
9. www.christymoore.com/lyrics/ninety-miles-to-dublin-town/, accessed 1 May 2018.
10. *Irish Independent*, 3 March 1981.
11. Ed Moloney, 'Censorship and the Troubles', in Mary Corcoran and Mark O'Brien (eds.), *Political Censorship and the Democratic State: The Irish Broadcasting Ban* (Dublin, 2005), p. 103.
12. Ibid., p. 53.
13. Ferriter, *Ambiguous Republic*, pp. 325–39.
14. Moloney, 'Censorship and the Troubles'.
15. *Irish Independent*, 11 April 1981.
16. Lee, *Ireland, 1912–1985*, p. 676.
17. www.thejournal.ie/state-papers-uk-1247297-Jan2014/, accessed 5 October 2018.
18. *The Guardian*, 16 June 2001.
19. John Jeremiah Cronin and Pádraig Lenihan, 'Wars of Religion, 1641–1691', in Jane Ohlmeyer (ed.), *The Cambridge History of Ireland*, vol. III: *1550–1730* (Cambridge, 2018), pp. 246–73.
20. *The Guardian*, 16 June 2001.
21. Carr, *Rule of the Land*, p. 207.
22. Ibid.
23. William V. Shannon, 'The Anglo-Irish Agreement', *Foreign Affairs* 64(4) (Spring 1986), pp. 849–70.
24. Ibid.
25. Garret FitzGerald, *All in a Life: An Autobiography* (Dublin, 1991), pp. 567–8.

26. NAI DT 2016/52/65, Meetings between Taoiseach Garret FitzGerald and British prime minister Margaret Thatcher, 6 December 1986.
27. FitzGerald, *All in a Life*, p. 570.
28. Paul Bew and John Bew, 'War and Peace in Northern Ireland, 1965–2016', in Bartlett (ed.), *Cambridge History of Ireland*, vol. IV, pp. 441–76.
29. *Irish Times*, 9 and 15 August 1986.
30. *Irish Times*, 17 January 1987.
31. Quoted in Bew and Bew 'War and Peace', p. 462.
32. NAI, 2017/10/8, Report of meeting attended by Noel Dorr and Lord Whitelaw, 6 February 1987.
33. Tom Wilson, *Ulster: Conflict and Consent* (London, 1989), pp. 271–3.
34. Liam de Paor, *Unfinished Business* (London, 1990), pp. 120 and 149–51.
35. John H. Whyte, *Interpreting Northern Ireland* (Oxford, 1990), pp. 243ff.
36. Ibid.
37. Colm Tóibín, *Walking Along the Border* (London, 1987), p. 9.
38. Ibid., p. 30.
39. Ibid., p. 32.
40. Ibid., pp. 47–9.
41. Carr, *Rule of the Land*, p. 24.
42. Eugene McCabe, *Heaven Lies About Us* (London, 2006 edn), p. 88.
43. Eugene McCabe, *Death and Nightingales* (London, 1992), p. 21.

6: No Victory for Either Tradition

1. Seamus Mallon, 'It was John Hume, not Sinn Féin who steered Northern Ireland to Peace', *The Guardian*, 20 November 2017.
2. *Irish Times*, 9 January 1991.
3. Eammon O'Kane, 'Anglo-Irish Relations and the Northern Ireland Peace Process: From Exclusion to Inclusion', *Contemporary British History* 18(1) (Spring 2004), pp. 78–99.
4. Shannon, 'Anglo-Irish Agreement'.
5. Alvin Jackson, *Ireland, 1798–1998* (Oxford, 1999), p. 393.

6. O'Kane, 'Anglo-Irish Relations'.

7. Tom Garvin. 'Deal marks beginning of the end for politics of total victory or total defeat', *Irish Times*, 25 May 1998.

8. Roy Foster, *Luck and the Irish: A Brief History of Change* (London, 2007), pp. 140–41.

9. The Belfast Agreement Referendums, *Irish Times* supplement, 25 May 1998.

10. Ibid.

11. Ibid.

12. Roy Foster 'New definition for what it means to be Irish', *Irish Times* 25 May 1998.

13. Jackson, *Ireland, 1798–1998*, p. 394.

14. Bew, *Ireland*, p. 550.

15. Brian Ó Caoindealbháin, 'Citizenship and Borders: Irish Nationality Law and Northern Ireland', *Working papers in British-Irish Studies* no. 68 (2006), Institute for British-Irish Studies, University College Dublin.

16. Cited in Diarmaid Ferriter, *The Transformation of Ireland, 1900–2000* (London, 2004) p. 658.

17. Chris Mullin, *A Walk-on Part: Diaries 1994–1999* (London, 2012), pp. 460–61.

18. Ibid.

19. Bartlett, 'Ulster 1600–2000: Posing the Question'.

20. John Coakley and Liam O'Dowd, 'The Transformation of the Irish Border', *Political Geography* 26 (2007), pp. 877–85.

21. Catherine Nash, 'Border Crossings: New Approaches to the Irish Border', *Irish Studies Review* 18(3) (2010), pp. 265–84.

22. Harris: 'Anglo-Irish Elite Co-Operation and the Peace Process', pp. 203–14; Elizabeth Meehan, '"Britain's Irish Question: Britain's European Question?": British–Irish Relations in the Context of European Union and the Belfast Agreement', *Review of International Studies* 26 (2000), pp. 83–97.

23. *Irish Times*, 10 December 2010.

24. Coakley and O'Dowd, 'The Transformation of the Irish Border'.

25. Nash, 'Border Crossings'; Andy Pollak, 'Interview on North-South Cooperation with the Taoiseach, Brian Cowen TD', *Journal of Cross Border Studies in Ireland* 5 (Spring 2010), pp. 11–20.
26. Diarmaid Ferriter, *Occasions of Sin: Sex and Society in Modern Ireland* (London, 2009), pp. 475–81.
27. *Belfast Telegraph*, 19 October 2011.
28. *Irish Examiner*, 21 March 2018.
29. Ibid.
30. *Irish Times*, 11 October 2011.
31. *Irish Times*, 24 January 2001.
32. *Sunday Times* magazine, 13 May 2018.
33. Ibid.
34. Carr, *Rule of the Land*, p. 75.
35. Reproduced in the *Irish Independent*, 22 June 2016.

7: Brexit, Backstops and Brinkmanship

1. *Irish Times*, 29 May 2018.
2. Nicholas Wright, 'Brexit and Ireland: Collateral Damage?', in Benjamin Martill and Uta Staiger (eds.), *Brexit and Beyond* (London, 2018), pp. 105–13.
3. Paul Routledge, *John Hume* (London, 1998), p. 56.
4. Tony Connelly, *Brexit and Ireland: The Dangers, the Opportunities, and the Inside Story of the Irish Response* (Dublin, 2017), p. 334.
5. *University Times*, University College Dublin, 5 February 2017.
6. Ian McBride, 'After Brexit, Northern Ireland politics will again be dominated by the border', *The Guardian*, 19 July 2016.
7. In an interview on *The World This Weekend*, BBC Radio 4, 30 October 2016.
8. Richard Humphreys, *Beyond the Border: The Good Friday Agreement and Irish Unity after Brexit* (Dublin, 2018) and *Irish Times*, 24 August 2018.
9. Bartlett, 'Ulster 1600–2000: Posing the Question'.
10. Diarmaid Ferriter, 'Ireland is back on the menu in Westminster', *Irish Times*, 17 June 2017.

11. Peter Leary, 'There are three ways out of the Irish border impasse', *The Guardian*, 1 March 2018.

12. *The Independent*, 8 December 2017.

13. Newton Emerson, 'We may need to hold a border poll just to clear the air', *Irish Times*, 6 September 2018.

14. www.thejournal.ie/article.php?id=4059433, accessed 20 June 2018.

15. https://inews.co.uk/news/politics/new-poll-finds-just-21-support-for-a-united-ireland-despite-fears-about-post-brexit-irish-border/, accessed 20 June 2018.

16. *Irish Times*, 31 July 2018.

17. Peter Shirlow, 'Peter Robinson has delivered a "wake up call" for Unionism', *Irish Times*, 31 July 2018.

18. John FitzGerald and Edgar Morgenroth, 'The Northern Ireland Economy', Dublin Economics Workshop, 14 September 2018; *Irish Times*, 18 September 2018.

19. Connelly, *Brexit and Ireland*, p. 258.

20. www.cawt.com/.

21. Connelly, *Brexit and Ireland*, p. 254.

22. *Irish Times*, Weekend News Review, 12 May 2018.

23. Wright, 'Brexit and Ireland'.

24. *The Guardian*, 25 August 2017.

25. *The Guardian*, 7 June 2018.

26. *Irish Times*, 26 August 2018.

27. *Irish Times*, 16 June 2018.

28. *The Times*, 30 March 2018.

29. Spike Milligan, *Puckoon* (London, 1963), pp. 44–81.

30. *Irish Times*, 13 July 2018.

31. *Sunday Business Post*, 22 July 2018.

32. Diarmaid Ferriter, 'It's hard to know what the DUP is about anymore', *Irish Times*, 6 October 2018.

33. *Irish Times*, 26 April 2018.

34. Carr, *Rule of the Land*, p. 48.

35. MacDonald, *Hard Border*, pp. 322–8.

36. Clare Dwyer Hogg, *Brexit: A Cry from the Irish Border*, narrated by Stephen Rea, www.ft.com/video/33264c1e-c744–4b24-bdb7-b89b09716517, accessed 28 September 2018.

37. *The Guardian*, 15 November 2018.
38. Jeremy Smith, *The Tories and Ireland 1910-1914: Conservative Party Politics and the Home Rule Crisis* (Dublin, 2010) pp. 5–7.
39. *Irish Times*, 17 November 2018.
40. *Sunday Times* magazine, 17 November 2018.
41. Butler, 'Crossing the Border'.
42. Kiely, *Counties of Contention*, p. 1.

Index